MW00944796

BOY DOES WORLD

BOY DOES WORLD

Fifteen Years of Bad Behaviors,
Bad Attitudes, and Happy Endings

Sean Bugg

iUniverse, Inc.
New York   Bloomington

Boy Does World
Fifteen Years of Bad Behaviors,
Bad Attitudes, and Happy Endings

iUniverse books may be ordered through booksellers or by contacting:

iUniverse
1663 Liberty Drive
Bloomington, IN 47403
www.iuniverse.com
1-800-Authors (1-800-288-4677)

Because of the dynamic nature of the Internet, any Web addresses or links contained in this book may have changed since publication and may no longer be valid. The views expressed in this work are solely those of the author and do not necessarily reflect the views of the publisher, and the publisher hereby disclaims any responsibility for them.

ISBN: 978-1-4502-4253-0 (sc)
ISBN: 978-1-4502-4254-7 (ebk)

Printed in the United States of America

iUniverse rev. date: 09/15/2010

For Cavin, the happiest ending of all.

Contents

Introduction

There are upsides to being a tramp.

Obviously, there's the sex. That's easy because, well, you're easy.

Then there's the retelling. The bad tricks. The ones that got away. The smart enough to sleep with, but too stupid to date. The stupid enough to sleep with you, but smart enough to lose your number. The giddiness. The scares.

It's all about the stories you get to tell after.

But I never expected, during my early years as a wannabe journalist in the nation's capital, that after a desultory stint covering federal tax and securities policy, I'd find my calling by way of a humor column about my sex life.

It began as a lark that I tossed off in an afternoon, a short story about my first time buying a sex toy. I wrote it sitting in my small apartment at the folding table I used for a desk, on which teetered precariously a behemoth PC with a spacious ten-megabyte hard drive and a monitor that displayed up to forty lines of amber-hued text.

I shared the story with a few of my friends. It proved popular in my little circle because, naturally, sex toys are funny. Sometimes even when you're using them, but we'll get to that a little later.

Months after, in early 1994, the essay worked its way into the hands of Randy Shulman, the editor of a small gay magazine that had recently launched in the city. By that point, I had essentially abandoned journalism for activism—after all those years as a young boy in the western Kentucky farmlands, I'd decided that if I was going to be gay, I might as well be as goddamned gay as I could be. So when I was offered a regular gig at *Metro Weekly* writing about dildos and dating, nightclubs and sex clubs, the timing happened to be very, very good.

Plus, after all those years dreaming of being a writer, it was too tempting to be given the chance to actually be a writer, even if I ran the risk of regretting what I wrote.

Thus was born "The Back Room," my weekly chronicle of life as a young gay man in the city navigating the perils and pitfalls of sex, boyfriends, ex-boyfriends, parties, discos, fashion disasters, and more sex. What I initially envisioned as an unholy cross-pollination of Miss Manners and early P. J. O'Rourke evolved over time into a place where I was as likely to write about my closeted gay youth as I was my latest foray into debauchery.

The funny thing is, I've never regretted it. I have a certain bullheadedness about me—something about my

Irish/German heritage, I suspect—that probably explains why, when confronted with a decade that told gay men to fear sex and intimacy, I decided to get as much sex and intimacy as I could.

Not like every hour of every day. I had to make a living, you know. But if I were to boil down those early days to one word, I'd have to choose "exuberant."

All of which gave me plenty of material to work with. Like I said, being a tramp has its upsides.

But being a tramp isn't a choice for a lifetime. A search for sex and intimacy implies a search for something a little more lasting than a whirlwind weekend or even a months-long romance. As my own life and priorities changed—and as life for gay men came to be less about fear of what might happen and more about hope of what might be—my stories changed. So while "The Back Room" ended in 1998, I kept writing columns and essays for *Metro Weekly*, my own little journalistic home.

What had started as a small column about being a tramp grew into a life as a happy and healthy gay man. And so a young country boy with a big dream got to see it come true—not exactly in the way I planned, but that's what makes life interesting.

BEFORE: HELLO WORLD

Open Secret

I knew two things about my seventeen-year-old self when I decided to attend a conservative, private Southern college where the students had a well-known antipathy toward homosexuals.

First, based on the evidence of my own body and mind, I knew that no matter how much I'd fought it and tried to change it, I was probably going to end up gay.

Second, I knew that I'd be able to keep it hidden for just four more years until I got out of college.

I was right about the first one.

Almost immediately after arriving at Washington and Lee University, I threw myself into the fraternity rush system. It being the mid-eighties, the beer and grain alcohol punch flowed freely through the frat houses where I pretty desperately wanted to find a place to fit in, a place to be the straight college guy I was expected to be.

Funny, then, that I can look at the yearbook picture of me and my Sigma Nu brothers standing on the front porch of the frat house later that year and count seven then-closeted gay guys—eight if I broaden my definition a bit to include the "just curious"—and that's without knowing much about the juniors and seniors. For a house of fifty-odd members, that put us well over the 10 percent homo average.

Lest anyone think this was an anomaly, I can make similar picks in the group pictures of some of the other fraternities, which should come as absolutely no surprise to anyone inside or outside the Greek system. The fraternities have to get their social directors, presidents, and national office staff members from somewhere.

I didn't join a fraternity to meet other gay guys—I joined so I wouldn't be recognized as one. But of course I was, because in a hothouse environment like a Washington and Lee frat with a bunch of other late-teen guys hopped up on hormones, beer, and collegiate freedom, your gaydar's going to start popping like a silver spoon in a microwave.

I was still a pledge as fall rolled in for the first semester of my freshman year. I found myself more and more fascinated with my pledge brother Jim, a shaggy-haired artist type from Maine, who loved to talk about weird-ass artsy and philosophical shit with a thick Northeastern accent that took me forever to get my Kentucky ears accustomed to. I was smitten.

I don't recall how, one night at a Sigma Nu party, the two of us worked our way through the pink-elephant-lined basement bar and into the shabby, secluded laundry room in the back corner of the house. I don't remember what we were talking about in our drunken and possibly high state, although I know I was enraptured. I do remember him sitting on the washing machine and me looking in his eyes and the two of us kissing and then my life becoming so very, very different.

I suddenly had a secret life. I was in love, not only with another guy, but with a pledge brother. Given the rank homophobia of many of my pledge brothers—the viciousness of which I wouldn't truly understand until a couple years later, a story for another day—it was a pretty dangerous secret. But it didn't matter. I was deliriously happy, surreptitiously spending the night in Jim's private dorm room, exploring all the things I'd thought I wouldn't know until well past college, learning how it felt to be held by someone you love who loves you back.

It wasn't easy. We both discovered how jealous each of us felt watching the other dancing and drinking and hanging with the girls we dated to keep up appearances. And no matter how much in love I might have been, I had to tamp it down hard whenever we were in public—never let my gaze linger too long, never let myself touch him in an extra-fraternal way, never let myself say something telling.

I was happy, and I think he was too, but only behind a closed door.

I took Jim home with me that year for winter break, and my whole family took a liking to him. How could they not? He was a slightly oddball charmer with a quick smile who always saw the best in people.

One afternoon, I took him for a walk through my grandfather's fields, taking pictures of muddy creeks, lightning-struck trees, and the occasional weathered animal bones. Walking across a railroad trestle that straddled the creek, we decided to take a low-angle picture of the railroad tracks receding into the horizon.

He sat on the tracks and I sat between his legs, leaning back on him to get myself low for the picture, the ground way below us, the wind blowing through the railroad ties, and the threat of snow in the air—and there I was under the open sky being held by Jim.

Things didn't stay perfect because, after all, we were college boys pretending to be things we weren't. We went on to become full brothers in the fraternity—because the universe has a sense of humor, my badge number turned out to be Lambda 1069—but we distanced ourselves from each other as we entered our sophomore year, a distance that only grew over time.

An unfair situation, but such is life. The comforting thing about having a first true love is that, by definition, it implies another love to follow, and for both Jim and me, that's been the case. He's found his love and happiness in Seattle, and I've found mine here in DC. Yet even in that happiness, I can't forget the secret moment when someone smiled at me and kissed me and I first fell in love.

A WORLD OF TROUBLE
(1994–1998)

Things You Won't Find on the Home Shopping Network

I realized over cocktails one night that my life had undergone a radical change of heretofore unknown proportions: I no longer joke about dildos. I have actual, serious discussions with friends about dildos, butt plugs, and various other anal-insertive devices.

For some reason, at an earlier age, I had thought of dildos as the last refuge of the undesirable, the one who couldn't get laid. Of course, I also thought I would look eighteen forever. Now, older and somewhat wiser, I know there are a plethora of uses for surrogate penises beyond the above.

Nothing particularly earth-shattering in all this, except for one thing: I had never bought a dildo.

On the basis of this realization (plus the fact that I found myself on a Saturday night without anything or anyone better to do), I resolved to buy a new friend, of the rubber sort. I didn't have any particular set of criteria in mind. Just something vaguely humanoid with no inflatable body attached.

I chose what I considered to be a reputable dealer and made the trek to Dupont Circle. The first thing to strike me on entering the store was the lack of other customers. This went against my assumption that the place would be swarming with guys picking up those last-minute items to make the evening just right.

I asked the guy behind the counter if things were usually a little busier on a Saturday night. "I think there's a big party tonight," he said. Socially humbled, I said no more and meekly moved to the back.

Not much to choose from back there, but having recently come off a two-and-a-half year hiatus from bottoming, I was somewhat unsure of my limits—though the double-headed number that looked to be as big as a bodybuilder's thigh seemed to be outside them.

I started with the butt plugs, of which there were three sizes: ballpoint pen, Mt. McKinley, and "just right." It seemed like a good idea to get something that would stay put and do its job with little help. However, for the purposes of self-amusement, I didn't see how putting something shaped like an elf's hat up my butt would help much in the fantasy department.

I wanted your average, everyday, flexible, lifelike, all-American dildo with testicles for a base, which left me with two choices: big and incredibly big. Not being a complete size queen (and not wanting to test my limits that quickly), I settled for merely big.

It's too bad dildo shopping can't be more like car shopping. How hard would it be to have a few floor models on display so you can take a little spin and see how it handles? Granted, the dressing rooms would be interesting, and some people may have hygiene concerns. But placing some condoms around would solve that problem and send a safer sex message to boot.

I finally found one that seemed suitably lifelike and within the realm of physical capacity. While gently squeezing it to test the resilience, I had a brief, yet terrifying, vision of Mr. Whipple brandishing a riding crop. I shook the thought, took the package of pleasure from its hook, and proceeded to the register.

After paying the guy behind the counter and deciding not to ask where the party might be, I walked home with my new friend tucked discreetly in a paper bag. On the way, half of me chattered that everyone on the street had X-ray vision and thought what a loser I was on a Saturday night. The other half wanted to rip the machine-made manhood free from its bag and wave it playfully in the faces of passers-by. Thoughts like these keep my therapist in business.

I finally made it home without screaming my sexual proclivities to the world (that night at least). My new friend has found a good home on the closet shelf. I'm not going into further details, as some parts of my life remain private. Besides, I need something to talk about over cocktails.

Trick Etiquette

As a faithful reader of Miss Manners, I've anxiously awaited her pronouncement on one social phenomenon that affects me so directly: trick etiquette. However, she has chosen not to answer my inquiries, even when I used my best stationery. Her deafening silence leaves me with no other option than to develop my own structure for graciousness for yet another category of overnight guests.

In the interest of politeness, you and your potential new friend must perform certain ceremonial functions before leaving the club (or bar, bathroom, bushes, etc.). This includes gauging the compatibility—and safety—of the potential trick.

Helpful Etiquette Hint No. 1: Be subtle with your questions. For instance: "When you were in elementary school, did they pick you up in a big bus or a little bus?"

Both parties must clearly state their expectations for the expedition. Nothing perturbs me more than getting halfway through the evening's festivities only to be asked, "You want to *what*?"

Helpful Etiquette Hint No. 2: It's always more polite to deflect an unexpected request graciously. For example: "I'm so sorry, I seem to be all out of matches. Do you like Cool Whip?"

I always offer a trick a minimum of one glass of water as soon as we walk through the door. Are other refreshments required? A Diet Coke, vodka tonic, or light beer is always appropriate. Offering other treats from your kitchen or from what you have left over from the bar is purely up to your discretion. However, it is rude to use all the treats without offering.

I have had the unfortunate experience of bringing a trick home only to turn on a fluorescent light and realize what a disastrous misjudgment I have made. Although one's first instinct may be to quickly devise some excuse involving a forgotten business deal and a late flight to the West Coast—one should always project an aura of success—it is an urge best left alone.

Helpful Etiquette Hint No. 3: The only polite course of action is to turn off the lights and engage in a brief-as-possible act of mercy sex. Hell, one never said etiquette was easy.

But what *do* you do when you realize too late that you have chosen unwisely, and you find yourself dozing off with your mouth open and your legs wide? Go for the quick finish, and then explain that you have a nasty phobia about sharing your bed and are prone to kicking, punching, and biting while sleeping.

Sean Bugg

Helpful Etiquette Hint No. 4: Try not to hurt his feelings. Don't tell him he must leave because you can't face your roommate's laughter when you take him downstairs in the morning.

If, on the other hand, your trick was especially fulfilling, keep him around for brunch. That way you can show him off to your friends. When it comes to men, it's always polite to show others you have something that they don't. But exercise caution; it's never fun to discover that all of one's friends have already traveled that particular highway.

Helpful Etiquette Hint No. 5: Thank-you notes are not required, regardless of what your mother taught you.

Happiness Is a Warm Bottom

A friend of mine in the Midwest once asked me what's the fastest way to become a bottom. "Easy," I said. "Move to DC."

I know that some queens get their g-strings in a bunch when this topic comes up. "But I am a top! I am!" Right. And Rush Limbaugh is my biggest fan. I've been to parties where a rumor starts that a certain blond, just-out-of-college boy is a top, and suddenly three-fourths of the revelers are following him around as if he were the Pied Piper.

Although DC does have a surplus of bottoms, as does every other city with more than two gay male citizens, I would like to dispel the seeming stigma by pointing out the many advantages of the passive persuasion.

To begin with, bottoms party better. You can party all night long and still have fun with your trick. Who needs an erection when he already has one? Even better, if you're feeling a little sleepy (never, never tired), you can sneak in a quick power nap. If he's like most tops, he'll never know the difference.

What does the resourceful bottom do when he brings his trick home, only to discover the guy's facial structure doesn't hold up in residential lighting? Easy. Just spend the whole sordid adventure face-down (you may want to get a printed pillowcase with a shot of your favorite porn star to keep your mind busy). Just make sure he doesn't try to sneak in any of those sideways kisses.

Let us not forget the most important physiological advantage of going bottom: The penis doesn't have a prostate. How anyone could go through life without stimulating this organ-gift-of-the-gods is beyond me. But once you've had it tickled, you'll never go back.

Since it has already been established that DC's queer bars and clubs are rife with bottoms seeking tops, there is the problem of what to do when your search comes up empty. You'll be happy to know that a bottom's options for self-pleasure are almost endless.

Just take a look at the toy section of your favorite supply shop. Dildos, butt plugs, rubber fists, battery-operated wriggling things, and a plethora of other choices line the walls (I still haven't figured out the instructions for some of them, and I'm not sure I want to know). The inventory in the store is empirical evidence enough of the bottom surplus.

It's even socially acceptable to own a dildo, perhaps having it on discreet display in your home (a little butt-plug basket in the bathroom always adds charm). But having a plastic, life-size Butt-Boy Bob sitting in the corner of your bedroom still carries a certain social price.

So what do you do the next time you hear that plaintive whine, "But I am a top!"? Take the confused queen home and fully demonstrate the benefits. After all, the primary advantage of being a bottom is you can have your cake and eat it too.

The Shape of Things to Come

Being a male teenager, whether hetero or homo, means two things.

First, there's the near-uncontrollable obsession with having sex, the result of all those hormones that scare the hell out of you the first time your penis shoots the white stuff while you're locked in the family bathroom.

Second is the definitely uncontrollable obsession with one's own penis, generally revolving around the question, "Is it big enough?" (The answer to which is generally, "If you have to ask …")

Fortunately for all those straight men out there, straight women have evolved the uncanny ability to say, "Honey, it's just right," and sound like they actually mean it.

We gay men, on the other hand, don't have any such gentle white lies to help us conquer our fears. After all, we're having sex with guys—and when was the last time you were able to suppress that little sigh of dissatisfaction upon finding a teeny one hiding behind those Calvins?

But aside from all this, what caused me the most anxiety as a young boy was not really the size, but the shape. Or, to be more specific, the direction it pointed.

While what few erect penises I had seen in *Hustler* and other illicit pornography pointed straight out or hung somewhat downward, mine pointed straight to the sky like a whacked-out dowsing rod predicting a thunderstorm. Granted, it made for a great towel rack after showering when I needed both hands free to deal with my hair, but it made me feel somewhat deformed.

So you can imagine my glee when I finally saw a porno in which one of the male stars sported an angle of erection that threatened to put out his own eye. It was the proof I needed that my penis wasn't deformed but very enthusiastic.

Of course, the world of porn is not the best place to study the field of penile geometry, particularly gay porn. Just as a hairy-chested man stands out as an anomaly (with the exception of Colt films*), penises with distinguishing characteristics other than size are few and far between.

It seems that only in real life do you run into a penis that signals a sharp turn to the left in the middle of the road. What puzzles me is the reaction this type of penis gets from many men—maybe they have some

_____

*   In the years since I wrote this, bear culture sprang up as a response to the plucked-and-shaved body fascism hairy men perceived in the twink-dominated gay world. Then bears started going to the gym and ended up as neatly-trimmed body fascists, so the great merry-go-round of life continued.

unexamined fear that the slightly bent member might cause them some internal damage. You'd think, after all that practice, their love canals would be callused enough to handle a boomerang.

Now that I'm grown, the curves and angles of man's best friend no longer give me pause. The only shape issue that I've been concerned about over the past few years has been those particular members that start out big at the top and end up small at the bottom. I've never been able to reach a level of comfort when it comes to sitting on the fleshy version of a giant Tootsie-Pop.

Queers to Watch Out For

W henever hundreds of gay men pack into a bar with one thing on their minds (okay, two things, cocktails and men), certain sticky social situations are bound to arise. Face it, as with most human beings, queers do not naturally get along with everyone, even other queers. This is most true of myself when the competition for a boyfriend becomes intense.

More importantly, there are some queers who are not only impossible to get along with, but from whom you should keep your distance at all times (preferably a minimum of five hundred yards or ten city blocks, whichever comes first).

Number One: Anyone Singing Show Tunes (unless you're in a piano bar, which is another problem entirely).

If you don't escape the clutches of this Judy Garland-loving warbler, you'll find yourself trapped in an overly decorated high-rise condo, listening to the original cast recording of *Oklahoma!* and gazing at a vintage collection of *Playbills*. He may want to show you how hip he is by popping in his copy of Ethel Merman's disco album.

Important note: This advice also applies to karaoke nights. It goes double for anyone who does "New York, New York."

Number Two: Guys Whose Soloflex Bodies Seem to be Augmented with Strategically Placed Padding.

If the biceps underneath his tight sleeves look too good to be true, keep an eye out—when they migrate to his forearm as he twirls on the dance floor, there is a definite problem.

Like pre-teen girls stuffing bras, some men will go to ridiculous lengths to create the illusion of a penis. I still have nightmares about the guy I took home one strange evening—his jeans turned out to be hiding an oversized cup and a balled-up pair of athletic socks. Did he think I wouldn't notice? Remember what they say about Depends adult diapers: They're not just for bladder control problems anymore.

Number Three: Any Queer Boy Whose First Question Is "So, Buy Me a Drink?"

This may be okay if the drinks cost a dollar or less. Otherwise, look at it as the shape of things to come, especially if he says, "I only drink Absolut and tonic." After displaying your largesse in his favor, you will never get him out of your house—he'll be too enthralled by the fact that you have both a couch and a coffee table to go back to his efficiency apartment with the miniature stove and broken futon.

Number Four: Any Queer Boy Whose Second Question Is "So, What Do You Do?"

Actually, the question isn't so bad when it's not immediately followed by a blatant attempt at networking for a new job. Of course, if your career doesn't meet his standards, the conversation will stop short.

In general, don't waste your time with career-inquiry boys. If he goes home with you, he'll spend the whole night thinking, "I hope his income is six figures," or, "I love that vase. It'll go great with my table."

Number Five: People Who Don't Understand that You Go to the Rail to Order Drinks.

Bar space is just that: space. Use of the bar space is a privilege, not a right. So, if someone elbows you out of your hard-earned perch to order a cheap beer, feel free to accidentally spill your drink on his new wool sweater. Don't fool yourself, regardless of how gorgeous he may be, he will never grasp the concept of separate toothbrushes.

Number Six: Guys Who Hang Around in the Bathroom Waiting for an Invitation to Pleasure in the Stall.

During each of my bathroom trips on a recent night out, a strange man made goo-goo eyes and small hand gestures for me to join him in the Romper Room. A piece of advice to him and his brethren: go somewhere darker. It might help.

Number Seven: A-Listers.

This is the queer most likely to ask, "What does your father do?" Odds are the A-lister's own daddy would have a Fortune 500 heart attack if he knew of his heir's orientation. There are two ways to get rid of an A-lister: act more effeminate than he, or claim poverty.

And, finally, the one queer to really watch out for: Anyone who looks like that old guy who lived down the street in your hometown and kept a stack of *Playgirls* in his garage.

I Like It, Really I Do

S ome of my friends and acquaintances have suggested that I am—how shall I put it—just a tad bit cynical. "Doesn't anything make you happy?" they ask, even though Miss Manners clearly outlaws this type of personal inquiry. I suppose putting my private life on public display allows a suspension of the rules.

The answer to that question, in case you were wondering, is an unequivocal "Yes, there are things that bring joy to my life." And, for the more than curious, here they are, in slightly abbreviated form.

Free cocktails.

Nothing improves my mood faster than a complimentary vodka tonic sailing across the bar. The key to receiving them, of course, is not to expect them (i.e., don't expect anyone trying to pick you up to buy you one—but if he doesn't, ditch him).

Here's some advice for those just starting their quest for free drinks. Always drink in a group. When everyone is down to two swallows, excuse yourself to the bathroom. When you return, a cocktail will have magically appeared. This system also has the advantage of making you look less like an alcoholic, a tough job in a gay bar.

Porno movies.

Whether it's a Kristen Bjorn "Look Ma, no hands" epic, a Falcon "Take that big dick" fantasy, or a Puppy Productions "Do I really have to kiss him?" number, nothing keeps me glued to the couch like two or more guys going at it on the big screen with stereo Surround Sound. The best thing is that pornos can provide education as well as stimulation. I would never have tried some things without seeing them first in *The Abduction*.

Two types of porno movies fail to arouse me: solo and amateur. Why watch some guy do something I already do when I'm alone (and I've already discovered the nine billion ways and places to do it)? And amateur videos only remind me of some of the sillier tricks from my past, where my so-called partner thought the orgasm was his exclusive domain.

Cigarettes.

When I have a cocktail in one hand, what goes better in the other than a cancer stick? Well, one thing is better, but that's not allowed in most bars. I've discovered that cigarettes also provide a valuable social service by chasing away people I don't want to talk to in the first place.

Fortunately, since queers are one of the last marketing niches for cigarettes aside from white, slightly overweight, sixteen- to twenty-four-year-old females, the cigarette companies will give me free watches, hats, and canoes to increase my butch quotient.

A-listers.

Watching these guys fight for position on the social ladder provides me with more entertainment than *Rescue 911* and *Melrose Place* combined. I get the giggles when reading the names on the host committee for the latest black-tie fundraiser. And just when I thought they couldn't get any funnier, along comes another conversation about *Architectural Digest.* Being low-class never felt so good.

One-shot lube packs.

Convenient, fast, and ready to travel, lubricant pillows are the most useful American product to come down the pike since Handi Wipes. The only improvement I can think of would be to make the containers bio-degradable so the little plastic carcasses won't litter parks and rest areas.

Things that make me laugh.

Just about everything and everyone.

The Well-Prepared Bedside Table

After a long night of exchanging meaningful glances across a smoky room, making semi-intelligent introductory conversation, and positioning my body to send the message, "Yes, I would love to go home with you," I often find myself disappointed when arriving at the chosen place.

I don't care if the bedroom is tidy. In fact, if a bedroom is too clean, I begin to worry about underlying obsessions. What drives me crazy is the lack of preparation for a late night/early morning *pas de deux*. Any self-respecting, sexually-active queer boy should have the following items within handy range if he intends to make a go of the local trolling scene.

Item One: Condoms.

Whether you plan to pretend you're a top for the night or to let the bottom who lives inside you make a cameo appearance, you'd better have these handy. Novelty condoms that glow in the dark, have a witty slogan on the side, or boast stenciled inch marks don't cut it. I still remember the night a guy tried to use a Rough Rider on me. Whoever thought that making condoms out of no-slip bathtub liners would be erotic?

By the way, if you keep Magnum extra-large sheaths by the bed, be sure your equipment can fill them. Otherwise, you'll have trouble making your dirty talk heard over the sound of your trick's laughter.

Item Two: Lubricant.

It's not the same as spit-and-go, but it has enough advantages to make it worth the investment. You can keep a small basket of lube packets, but most queers seem to prefer the full bottle by the bed. Try to get a model with a pump—not only can you refill it, it reduces the risk of accidents. Standard, phallic-shaped lube bottles can get slippery, and if you squeeze too hard without a good grip on the thing you could put out an eye.

Item Three: Towels.

Those of us who haven't given in to the body-shaving craze will thank you for this little convenience. I don't care if it's a bath, hand, or beach towel, or even a box of tissues. I just don't want to wake up in the morning feeling like someone squirted an entire bottle of Krazy Glue on my chest.

Don't go overboard on this. The implications of having a stack of clean, white, neatly-folded towels on top of the nightstand will definitely cut down on your chances of a second date.

Item Four: Poppers.

Only bring these out if you're sure you both have the coordination to use them. They're great for easing your way into certain situations, but air fresheners they're not (unless you consider the smell of three-week-old, used athletic socks exciting—which, I suppose, is a possibility).

As to the negative health benefits of poppers, they can melt a contact lens in one second flat. If they made you happier and healthier, they would replace Prozac and All Bran as our culture's favorite cure-all.

Item Five: Toys.

What do you do to save the evening when you find that you've brought home yet another top who turns out to be a bottom? Pull out a rubber surrogate from your bag of tricks. Your guest will be so happy you may even get a thank-you note later in the week. And you'll both be happier if you pull out a double-header, the Siamese twins of dildos.

Item Six: A Camera.

For those Kodak moments you'll want to treasure for years to come (it may be helpful if you keep a model-release form handy). If your sex life is particularly silly, consider installing a video camera and submitting the results to Fox as the lead segment on the new show *America's Bedrooms Exposed!*

Impaled on a White Picket Fence

Without fail, every time I find myself in a sexual interlude with a halfway-decent trick, my mind begins playing tricks of its own. Right after my boyfriend for the evening and I finish our festivities, my brain begins to extrapolate our future together from only his length, girth, and approximate age.

This type of relationship prognostication is the definition of "fraught with danger." Before I know it, I'm calling him two or three times a day, hanging near the door of the bar in the hopes he'll walk in, and making special trips to Nordstrom's so I'll look beguiling when I finally have that "chance" encounter.

Since I've been on the receiving end of these delusions as well, I know this fantasy syndrome is all too common. Fortunately, there are warning signs. Memorize them for the sake of your own mental stability.

Number One: I Wonder What He Likes for Breakfast?

This creepy little thought usually crops up about the time he rolls over and begins to snore. Will he like granola with yogurt and fresh fruit on top? What if he wants to go out for brunch? Before you know it, you'll be sneaking out of bed to run to the 7-Eleven and pick up buttermilk for your mother's famous biscuit recipe.

Number Two: Picturing Yourself at Dinner with Him.

Before this fantasy is over, you'll have already worked yourself into an anxiety attack about finding reservations at the "right" restaurant and ordering the correct wine with dinner. In extreme cases I've developed contingency plans for getting pieces of food unstuck from between my front teeth without him noticing.

Number Three: Picturing Yourself with Him at Social Functions.

The two of us will enter the room and everyone will pause with their vodka tonics halfway to their lips, thinking, "Oh my God, what a gorgeous couple! Why don't they share the wealth?"

My own personal variation on this is to combine it with the dinner fantasy and imagine us attending a state dinner at the White House.

Number Four: Should I Keep Talking to this Guy?

I know I'm in deep when I begin turning away potential tricks because I've married myself off in my mind, even though my "beloved" hasn't bothered to call me for a week. Nothing gets the hot boys coming after me faster than believing I have a boyfriend.

Much to my chagrin, however, I've found it tough to turn off the trick mentality. Even though I desperately want to keep a semblance of chastity for my potentially-betrothed, I find myself making the appropriate eye contact, smiling with clenched teeth at how fascinating it is to work on Capitol Hill, and automatically taking a proffered phone number with a little smiley face drawn at the end of the name.

Number Five: Picking out Shower Curtains and Dining Room Tables.

If, after all this, the relationship actually progresses to a second date, I begin comparing his furniture to mine, deciding whose couch we'll keep. During innocent walks around the neighborhood, I find myself memorizing posted phone numbers to call about vacant apartments, wondering if a two-bedroom would be big enough or if our combined incomes would allow us to rent a small house together (with a cute backyard for Fourth of July barbecues with all of our fabulous friends).

When you find yourself in the grips of this heinous syndrome, you may believe sanity will never return. But the symptoms will eventually subside. It usually takes about four to six weeks—add two weeks for every orgasm you have with him after the first date. I have a plea for all those wonderful men out there who may induce me to take a three-month journey down fantasy lane: Leave when you're done, don't bother to call me, and avoid me in the bars. I know how to deal with that.

It's good to keep life simple.

Jerked Around

I remember reading some time ago that men set the size of their sexual appetite by their rate of masturbation during childhood and adolescence. Of course, by this logic I wouldn't even be able to hold down a part-time job at McDonald's.

Like most other queers I know, I discovered the joys of self-fulfillment at an early age. This may have been helped along by the fact that my family's bathroom magazine basket always contained a copy of the Sears catalog and at least one magazine with a Jim Palmer Jockey ad.

This thirst for gratification, though not career-threatening, certainly has followed me into adulthood. Unfortunately, the population of the District cannot handle the demands of both me and the other denizens of the bars. As a result, I've become quite adept at meeting the physical calls of urgency that strike without notice. (I've always envied queens who work in private offices with locking doors.)

Though on the surface most acts of onanism would seem to be the same, there are four basic types of singular pleasure, independent of the time and location of the act.

Through the past, darkly.

How many times have you found yourself innocently going about your business when suddenly the memory of a particularly strenuous carnal act with a boyfriend from five years ago stampedes through your head? Your only option is to immediately run to the nearest bathroom to re-live the moment.

Searching through my mental databanks often provides my most fulfilling moments. Still, I sometimes have frightening flashes of my future as the sexual equivalent of the former high-school quarterback, with only the memory of an acrobatic evening in a Chicago bathhouse to make my life seem worthwhile. Needless to say, I try not to spend too much time dwelling on things to come.

Just one glance.

Another fun type of masturbation involves constructing complete mental fantasies about men you happen to see in a brief flash as they exit the Metro or saunter through the coffee shop. Nothing enhances a man's beauty more than not knowing exactly what he looks like.

One danger of this fantasy life is constructing a too-elaborate scenario of pleasure. Before you know it, you can have a complete mental dossier containing family background, college education, and current salary level from just a glimpse of a nicely rounded backside.

Better living through machines.

Mechanical aids and latex surrogates have the advantage of playing double duty—you can use them alone or with a friend. I only opt for these when my bank account won't allow me to cavort in the clubs in search of the real thing, but I have too much energy to go to bed before midnight on a Saturday.

The problem with using a single man's boyfriend is that the amount of preparation and clean-up adds up to more work than just grabbing a trick for the night (though, admittedly, you don't have to come up with creative ways to avoid giving out your phone number).

When a dildo seems like too much work.

When all else fails, and you just want to satisfy your body's urges so you can return to the other important aspects of life, such as earning a living, pornography is the answer.

The only question is which suits you better—videos or magazines. It comes down to deciding what you want to use your free hand for: work the remote or turn the pages.

Though I like to consider this a thorough listing, I'm sure some of you have additional categories you think should be included. However, not everyone has a spine equipped to handle the strain of auto-fellatio.

Get Out

The most vexing aspect of searching out a short-term mate while prowling the nightclubs is determining if his personality will mesh with yours for a minimum of five hours. This entails screening men you meet for the telltale signs that a romp together would not be in your best interests: idiocy, a propensity for instant attachment, and psychotic breaks waiting for a trigger.

The proper form for extricating yourself from someone who hasn't passed muster is to smile politely, excuse yourself to the bathroom, and never return.

But there are times when you can't predict disaster before it happens. I know of an unfortunate man who brought home a muscle queen from the Boy-Mart one Friday night. After a brief trip to the bathroom to prepare for love, he returned to the bedroom to find the muscular sprite lying face-down and naked on the bed, butt aimed to the stars.

"Make Tina stink," the gym-queen hissed over his shoulder.

While I've never brought home such an obvious case of someone who should have been left at the bar (or the nearest support group), I have had my moments. Who hasn't gotten a cute guy home only to discover that it would have been more fun to have a three-way with Danny DeVito and Rhea Perlman?

Assuming you decide to finish the task at hand, you're left with the dilemma of getting him out of your home. Fortunately, as always, I have developed some techniques to dissuade my mistakes from spending the night.

Your first attempt at removing an unwanted guest should be subtle. Remember, you just want to have your bed to yourself for the night, not make an enemy who may run around town giving inaccurate specs on your penile endowment. I prefer the old standby, "Boy, do I have to get up early in the morning. How about you?" If he has any clue at all, this should do the trick nicely.

However, there are some guys out there who need the assistance of a sixteen-ton weight to the head before they get the point. In that case, try some of the following not-so-subtle hints:

"I need to get to sleep now. I think your underwear is in the refrigerator."

"Honey, you can turn off the camera now."

"All I have for breakfast is Count Chocula and scrapple."

"I have bad dreams sometimes. Last night I ripped my pillow apart with my teeth."

I have found that, regardless of how convincing my attempt, some guys will still want to stay the night. Always take this as an urgent warning—if you don't get rid of him now, there's a chance you may end up having to buy a house with him.

Of course, the possibility remains that he did not leave because he wanted to avoid hurting your feelings. This duel of mercy leads to an awkward conversational dance, both of you attempting to avoid giving out a phone number, address, or any other personal information, while saying through a frozen smile, "I really had a good time."

In the end, this will be why you decide he's actually a really nice guy and you would like to see him again.

Duck and Cover

Perhaps the most exasperating situation a queer boy can experience is an uncontrolled obsession about an ex-boyfriend. And we have to face facts: since not all of us can have the last name Jackson-Paris, we will all be dumped at some point by someone we think we love. *

The most important step in dealing with an unwanted obsession is acknowledging the problem (don't panic—this is not a twelve-step program or anything to do with Jenny Craig). It helps to know the common signs that signal a descent into ex-boyfriend mania.

For example, no matter how hard you try, he keeps showing up in your nightly fantasies. Even though you dig further and further into your memory banks in search of some relatively un-embarrassing sexual exploit from your past, your mind boomerangs back to that night he took you out behind the bar and had his way with you

---

* The fact that Rod and Bob called it quits only proves the point.

by the Dumpster. Soon you will see his face in every magazine, underwear catalog, porno movie, or trick you bring home.

Another sure sign is when you find yourself constantly looking for him at every bar, club, and party you attend. Given the melodramatic, *Tales of the City*-type coincidences endemic to urban queer life, this will happen every time you walk out your front door. The trick to handling the situation is to prepare for the meeting before you ever leave the house. Some would say the solution is to stay home alone when wallowing in self-pity, but I've always believed in sharing the best of myself with others.

Your first impulse upon seeing the object of your unreturned affection will most likely be to run to the women's room to fully enjoy your nervous breakdown. If you manage to suppress this (and have enough cheap cocktails), your next urge will be to storm right up to him and demand to know why he decided to completely ruin your life.

This tactic is dangerous because most people forget the first rule of announcing personal problems in public: you will have no awareness of your lack of volume control, thereby informing the entire establishment of your inability to find sexual fulfillment.

All Glenn Close jokes aside, thoughts of revenge will become a constant in your life. While the idea of showing him exactly how tight that cock ring can fit may be an entertaining fantasy, you should remember that the odds of getting off on an insanity plea are much lower than you think. And with the advent of caller ID, repeated calls and hang-ups have become a forgotten art form.

The final, worst-case scenario is to obsess about a boyfriend who has decided to continue your relationship as "just friends." This usually entails going out together socially and smiling with clenched teeth and bitten tongue at every person who asks, "Are you two back together?"

Never, never, never agree to this type of situation. Before you know it, he'll meet a cute guy (who will never be as cute as you, of course) and leave you on your own. The jealousy will boil up from your depths, leading to an explosion of bile that could very well clear the bar.

The only way to block him out of your mind is to keep him at the greatest distance possible. One good way to get distance is to buy him a one-way ticket to the opposite coast. However, not everyone can afford this, and the thought of him having more fun while he's away from you may be too much to bear.

Earning a Reputation

Over the past few years of putting together tips and guidelines for living the queer life, I've found that my reputation has grown by leaps and bounds. But my increasing reputation, otherwise known as notoriety, has raised a number of questions I believe I should answer for the benefit of other reputation-impaired queers.

To start, what is a reputation and how does it apply to your life? The only answer I've come up with is the same as the judicial definition of pornography: I know it when I see it. In essence, if people say things about you like "He's a great guy," or "He'll do anything for a friend," you don't have a reputation. If, however, you pass a patio establishment in your local queer neighborhood and every patron begins swapping stories about your previous evening's spectacularly silly sexual escapade, then you have a reputation.

Society often views reputations as the domain of the "bad girl." But in our gay-male-only culture (I'm speaking of queer boy sex here, so no letters telling me I'm exclusionary), someone has to bear the brunt of societal busybodies who are horrified at the thought of someone else having a good time.

Which brings me to the advantage of having a reputation: queer boys who have one consequently have more fun. When was the last time you heard an entertaining story about someone who conducts himself in a calm and gracious manner at all times, restrains himself from acting on natural impulses beyond basic sustenance, and always checks to see if he recognizes the face on the milk container? I get more entertainment out of *Full House* reruns. (Another advantage to having a reputation is that even if people don't like you, at least they know your name.)

And yet, even with all the wonderful reasons for making the reputation a part of your personality repertoire, I must give warning of the basic rule of reputations:

They are rarely, if ever, based on truth.

Try as I may, I have not found a way around this rule. Therefore, if you are dealing in the creation of your own reputation, your only choice is to beat everyone to the punch. After all, one of the fastest ways to get people to believe falsities about me is to provide the falsities myself.

The great American tradition of stretching the truth is the most practical tool available for shaping a reputation. People never believe the simple truth anyway, so think of embellishment as a way to make the factoids of your life more palatable for general consumption.

By embellishment, I mean techniques such as multiplying your sexual statistics by a factor of five, particularly when telling stories about last night's trick. However, do not take this as license to embellish things such as resumes or salaries, which may be verified or disproved at very inopportune moments (for example, the boy you've impressed with your high-level position makes a surprise visit to your workplace and finds you wearing an apron and paper hat).

I firmly believe that the bad reputation actually is a good thing. Still, my best attempts at using outrageousness to form my public identity sometimes fall short of what the public itself can devise. Just the other night, when a potential trick hinted that he had "heard" about me, I asked him to elaborate.

"Well, you're an untamable bottom," he said.

I couldn't have made up anything better.

Broke Down

Is it just me, or has anyone else noticed how expensive being queer actually is? I've heard that gays make about $10,000 more per year than the average straight person, but I haven't noticed that extra money in my account. Apparently, my day-job boss hasn't seen that statistic yet.

So, in the interest of finding an excuse not to spend my money on anyone but myself, I've been doing some thinking on where my money goes.

The Necessities.

Before I bother with the rent, utilities, or food, I have to deal with the essentials: condoms, lube, and all the accessories that make life fun. Of course, condoms don't really count as a financial burden—if you hang out in the right places, someone will give you a handful for free. Lube, however, can make a major dent in your pocket, particularly if you take home too many of those lube-a-holics who stop every thirty seconds to slick things up a little (I keep hoping the manufacturers will take a cue from Downy and offer refills in small, recyclable cardboard boxes).

If you intend to extend your sex life beyond vanilla, you'd better ask for a pay raise now. By the time you buy a wide enough selection of latex lovers to satisfy the most finicky trick (and pick up a couple of cute leather-and-chain outfits) your minimum monthly payment will be higher than your yearly salary.

The Bait.

If you want to go out and find that husband, at least for the night, you have to have something to offer, right? Take a look at any advertisement targeting queers—I'm convinced that the economic recovery was fueled by the overpriced trinity of tanning salons, gyms, and underwear sold in boxes featuring impossibly beautiful bodies. *

Once you've paid for your package, you have to buy the gift wrap. And trust me, few things will empty your purse faster than a trip to the current high-fashion mecca for gay men.

Cocktails.

Buying cocktails for people you want to meet is a venerable tradition, but it's one that is far too expensive to continue (unless drink prices are a dollar and under, a good bet in our besotted nation's capital). Anyway, my success rate in meeting guys by sailing a drink across the

---

* Gay men of the twenty-first century unite! Your stylish wallets and narcissistic tendencies constitute the economic rebirth of a nation.

bar has been negligible. Perhaps if I got up the nerve to talk to the recipients of my largesse, I might have more luck.

The Big Night Out.

It doesn't matter how much you plan, budget, and hide twenty-dollar bills in your socks—you are going to spend a fortune when you go out to clubs. I have walked out my door on Saturday night with the exact, calculated amount needed for cab, cover, and cocktails, only to come home with five fifty-dollar money machine receipts in my pocket.

So, as I live check to check with little or nothing left over in the bank, I have no choice but to fall back on the line I hear most often as I languish on my barstool: "So, buy me a cocktail?"

Broke Up

My former roommate, who will forever occupy a particularly warm place in my heart, would skillfully and gleefully intercept calls from my soon-to-be-ex-boyfriends. "Sorry, he died. Send a plant." *Click*. Unfortunately, this particular technique isn't always the best way to handle the dumping process. For one thing, if used too often, your apartment will end up looking like a small botanical garden.

We've all had to deal with relationships in which, after two weeks (or two months or two years), we find ourselves looking across the dinner table, suppressing thoughts of stuffing all the rolls into his constantly jabbering mouth.

Your first attempts at unburdening yourself should center on giving him the idea to leave of his own volition. This can often be accomplished through subtle hints such as clumsily erasing his name from your speed-dial list or forgetting to mention that you changed your phone to an unlisted number.

Sometimes, though, the same thick skull that made you want to dump him in the first place effectively prevents any message from getting through. When this happens, which is the majority of the time, you have the obligation to make things clear.

Avoid any phrase that remotely resembles, "Let's just be friends." At least give the poor guy the dignity and pride of knowing he warranted a complex and elaborate excuse for the breakup.

A time-honored and functional excuse is the difference in age. Usually, this takes the form of "I feel guilty having a relationship with you. There's so much for you to experience and do." This technique can backfire, however, if you constantly romp through bars with queers-in-training who look as if they just came from their baccalaureate ceremony.

The best thing about this excuse is its flexibility: "There's so much *I* want to experience and do." You'd better hope your boyfriend bought it when you lied about your age (and that a hair plug doesn't fall into your soup during the break-up dinner).

If you and your boyfriend are near the same age, jump to the work excuse. "I'm just so focused on my career right now, with that promotion I want and all the projects I have to complete, it's not fair to you to have a relationship where I can't give you the attention you deserve." This excuse is best used while wearing a constantly beeping pager or ringing phone.

Be warned: If you use this excuse, you must stay at home every night for at least two weeks. It will destroy your credibility when your ex sees you taking advantage of every weeknight drink special in town.

None of these options may apply if the boyfriend you're trying to dump actually shares your abode. If this is the case, there's only one thing you can do...

Surprise him on his birthday with a solo vacation in Puerto Rico. When he returns, surprise him with his belongings on the sidewalk and new locks on the doors.

Stopped Cold

Has your credit card begun to wilt from buying the latest issue of *First Hand*, *Jock,* and every other porno magazine in a ten-mile radius? Have you committed to memory the names of every crew member for each Falcon movie at the local video store? Do you get frequent-flyer miles for your trips to the bathhouse?

Whether it's a phase of the moon, a result of bio-rhythms, the action of the zodiac, or simply the arrival of spring, most queer boys will go through phases of near-uncontrollable hormonal activity. If unchecked, your frenzied search for sexual fulfillment will soon have everyone crossing to the other side of the street when they see you making your rounds.

Not that there's anything inherently wrong with this. Who hasn't been in a relationship where you're continually trying to stoke a dead fire while praying for a sudden surge in testosterone? But there are nights (or weeks, or months) when you lie on the couch wishing your penis would shut the hell up and let you watch TNT's Dolph Lundgren marathon in peace.

To help fight these impulses, I've developed a few techniques guaranteed to take the fire out of your quest.

Step One: Clean the Bedroom.

Being a bit of a procrastinator, I have been known to leave my apartment for the evening without first taking care of that three-foot stack of clothes surrounding my bed, emptying the ashtrays, or putting away the scattered lube-and-condom kits. As a result, I've found a strong correlation between the state of my bedroom and potential for it being used.

In other words, the messier the room, the hotter the boy who wants to see it. The more I vacuum, dust, and launder to turn my den of iniquity into a husband trap, the less likely it is to see a suitor.

Step Two: Hygiene? Who Needs Hygiene?

Try to go for three or four days without taking a shower or using any of those special gifts you received with your purchase at the Lancôme counter. If you can't keep away from the cute boys, this will at least keep them away from you. With the abundance of hyper-hygiene in boy bars, most men will consider you ripe if you miss one shower and a shave.

Step Three: Eat, Eat, Eat.

Two burritos, a Super Big Gulp, and a box of Twinkies twice a day for one week can do the trick nicely. The constant question, "Are you gaining weight?" will do wonders for killing your sex drive. If you start running around the bar in a tank top and hot pants, you may kill everyone else's too.

Step Four: Knock Yourself Out.

When the urge has become overwhelming, masturbate continuously for an hour—that should wear you out enough to get some sleep. This technique works particularly well if it's 4:00 AM and your sundial is reading high noon. Be sure to drink plenty of fluids. But don't resort to drastic measures like saltpeter. Why try to avoid playing with others if you can't play with yourself?

In the end, there are a multitude of opportunities to avoid having sex. Still, one technique stands out above all others as the sure-fire, money-back-guaranteed way to avoid having a guest in your bed.

There's no one left in the city you haven't done.

After Hours

I've noticed that when a club begins to clear around 4:00 AM, there's always a crowd that refuses to give up and go home to bed. Instead, with the desire to continue the stimulating conversation (and have that one last chance at getting lucky), they decide to check out an after-hours party.

As with most other forms of social interaction, some rules must be followed to ensure that a host will risk having another one the following weekend.

Invitations.

Custom dictates that an invitation cannot be given until after 2:00 AM. All invitations must be verbal. Pre-printed invitations kill the spontaneity associated with these events. Besides, half the fun of an after-hours party is trying to remember where it is, and then trying to prove you were invited.

The bane of the after-hours existence is the uninvited guest, which usually comes in a pack of ten. Handle these creatures preemptively at the club by giving them invitations to someone else's apartment on the other side of town (for example, your ex-boyfriend's place).

What do you do when a friend decides to host yet another after hours when his last three parties have been disasters? Send him home to get the place ready. When he's gone, change the location.

Essentials to have on hand.

Planning for the party goes against the letter and spirit of after-hours law. Guests should feel as if they are making a party out of whatever and whoever is available. The only additions they need are what they have left over from the bar and what they can pick up at the 7-Eleven.

Still, there are basic essentials that all party queers should have on hand: an ice maker, Diet Coke, tonic, a large bottle of cheap vodka—hide the Stoli—and a collection of McDonald's movie tie-in cups. Don't underestimate the importance of owning plastic glasses; otherwise, all your good crystal will be smashed by some twisted queen who's moving to Miami in the morning.

Also essential is some form of electronic entertainment, preferably audio (leave the vibrator under the bathroom sink where it belongs). Music provides the best background for rehashing the entire evening. If the television must be on, mute the volume. A strung-out group of queens transfixed at 5:00 AM by a Thighmaster infomercial is a terrifying sight.

Porno movies with no sound make an excellent backdrop for an after-hours, especially when the conversation has become particularly insipid, and you want to break everyone's concentration.

This is what they mean by open house.

Check your bedroom, bathroom, and closets periodically for those unexpected couplings and triplings that can occur. If you are not careful, they may use all your lube, leaving you high and dry for your own private sunrise service with some guy whose name you can't remember, but he sure is cute.

You may want to take the precaution of locking the bedroom door. Some guests may think you are rude, but screw 'em, it's your house. Besides, there's nothing worse than rolling over onto a wet spot you had nothing to do with.

Leftovers

E ven though I came out of it years ago, my closet still manages to throw out surprises on occasion.

My usual morning routine consists of over-sleeping by about forty-five minutes, leaving me fifteen minutes to shower, shave, and scream as I try to wrench a comb through my hair. Then I have to attempt to get dressed for work while balancing a cup of coffee and a cigarette (I don't start pretending to be healthy until mid-afternoon).

I rarely pay attention to which clothes I happen to grab from the closet—unless I've outgrown them, which is a bitter topic for another day. Due to my inability to set a regular time to do laundry, I tend to reach the dregs of my wardrobe rather quickly. For this reason, I often find myself on the way to work, beyond the point of no return, when I suddenly realize why the shirt I'm wearing doesn't quite look right on me.

It belongs to *him*.

At that point I know I should go home, call in sick, and spend my mental health day in bed. Instead, I dutifully make my way to my desk, where I can mope about that relationship gone bad for an entire day.

Looking at the remains of my past boyfriends is like looking at the remains strewn on the beach after a shipwreck—although my love life is perhaps more appropriately rendered as *Gilligan's Island*. I tend to over-pack, too.

Memories attach themselves to items—or is it the other way around? In either case, I can't bring myself to throw away unclaimed items from my personal lost and found department. Perhaps it's a belief that the person may come back to claim it some day. Or maybe I hope that if I wash the damn thing often enough, the extra-strength Tide will get the invisible stains out.

Actually, clothing is a much better way to remember an ex-boyfriend than the traditional picture taken during one of those happy moments celebrating a holiday or lounging on the couch. Pictures force you to remember something in a precise, realistic way. But clothing memories are along the lines of smelling an apple pie like your granny used to bake. If you're in a good mood, you remember the way she always gave you an extra piece with vanilla ice cream on top. If you're in a bad mood, you remember how she chased you with a flyswatter after you took a chunk out of the pie with your grubby little hand.

Of course, it's not as if I'm grabbing all the souvenirs I can when I sense a relationship is about to hit the rocks;

plenty of my own things have wandered out of the house and into a new life.

I often begin a sudden search for that favorite shirt or tie, digging through the closet, checking under the bed, tearing apart the entire house, before remembering that it's across town in the closet of boyfriend number twelve. I can't bring myself to call and ask for it back; that might mean I would have to return those Doc Martens that fit me so well.

Love Bites

For all those out there who have asked if my columns are based on true stories (and, if so, how I can still manage to walk), let me reassure you that the following is *definitely* an adaptation of an actual incident, with certain names, dates, places, and acts changed to protect the innocent, not to mention what's left of my reputation.

I had to go to work last week with a hickey. Not the sort of hickey you gave yourself by sucking on your forearm in grade school, but a full-size, blood-clot-to-the-brain, grand-mal hickey roughly the size of Rhode Island. And even though I entered the office looking like the latest victim of Lestat, I couldn't bring myself to wear a turtleneck on the first ninety-degree day of summer.

Are people that surprised to see evidence that I have an active sex life (well, okay, semi-active), or at least engage in some obviously intense foreplay? Perhaps everyone wants to believe that I actually stay home and pretend my hormones don't exist, regardless what they may have heard about me.

Even more surprising was my embarrassment at being marked, which led me to create numerous ludicrous excuses:

"A rabid cat attacked me on the way to work."

"It was a bizarre gardening accident."

"I've never been able to tie a double Windsor."

"You know how it is when you try to shave and smoke at the same time."

I couldn't tell them the truth: "I met a really cute guy with more sticking power than Spider-Man."

We are all fortunate that other carnal activities don't leave telltale signs the next day. Imagine how much fun it would be to go to work with a big red exclamation point on your forehead the day after you finally put your legs in the air for your new boyfriend, or a lightning bolt emblazoned on your cheek after you pretend to be a top, or Greek letters on the bridge of your nose representing that little frat boy you picked up on your way home last night.

Although the constant stream of jokes over the course of the week almost pushed me into a psychotic break (this hickey has a longer half-life than plutonium), I'm not truly in a position to judge them.

I remember my high school business teacher coming to class one day with a fresh red spot on her neck. While she slowly and deliberately explained the advantages and disadvantages of single-proprietorship, my best friend and I speculated on what other area of her body might have markings of love. After much hushed discussion and accompanying diagrams in our notebooks, we decided the most likely candidate would be her big toe.

By the time I fell out of my desk laughing, my GPA had faltered and my career in business was stillborn.

In order to avoid a repeat of this week's neck fiasco, I've laid down a new rule regarding my activities: No marks from the shoulders upward. This should forestall any unseemly comments from my coworkers and friends. Just don't ask me to pull my shirt up anytime soon.

Doing Stonewall 25

J ust a few short hours after my arrival in New York, I found myself racing to cover a cucumber with twelve condoms.

I had come to participate in the National Lesbian and Gay Health Conference, which, along with just about every other queer organization in the nation, had conveniently scheduled its meeting in conjunction with the twenty-fifth anniversary of the Stonewall rebellion. For lower-level functionaries, such as myself, from gay organizations, this is the best way to travel.

For years, people had asked me, "How do you like such-and-such in New York?" To which I've always sheepishly replied, "Well, I've never been." From the reactions I've gotten, you'd think I had told them I was a virgin. So Stonewall 25 gave me the opportunity to look people straight in the eye, nod knowingly, and say "Oh, yes. It's fabulous!" (Note to day-job boss: I also learned a lot at the conference. Really.)

Of course, with approximately five gazillion queers running around Manhattan, my cavorting cannot possibly be taken as a true New York experience. As we Washingtonians know so well from the March on Washington, the true quality of a bar or club cannot be measured when block-long lines of vacationing Kentucky boys are waiting to be allowed in.

After extricating myself from the latex and cucumber workshop, I ventured out among the crowd at the Roosevelt Hotel. While the hotel employees described the Roosevelt as one of the best hotels in Manhattan, the conference attendees more accurately described it as a "Motel 6 with a nice lobby." Perhaps the employees had fond memories of the hotel's glory days, or they just saw *The Shining* one too many times. Since Leona's place was only a block away, I told everyone I met that my hotel was Helmsley-adjacent.

Tiring of the preliminary cruising in the lobby and the line of frantic hotel guests trying to check out to search for better accommodations, I retired to my room. Aside from the hole in the carpet and the lack of a working phone or television, it was relatively comfortable.

Unfortunately, it had a shower by Sybil that switched from ice cold to scalding hot in a matter of milliseconds. A visit from Mrs. Bates would have been more relaxing. By the grace of God, the air conditioner worked. As the week wore on and the stay grew more tedious, my friends and I made enemies of the hotel staff by running past the gigantic check-in line yelling, "Hotel Hell! Hotel Hell!"

Of course, I must admit, it's the only hotel I've patronized that turned a blind (or sleeping) eye to a 6:00 AM party in the lobby. Another plus was the conveniently unlocked maid's office on my floor—a handy space when five people are crashed in your double room and you need a place to make nice with your trick, pronto.

The Michelin Guide doesn't give these sorts of details.

My exploration of New York began in the West Village with an early evening trip to the Monster, a bar apparently named in honor of its interior decorator. Encased over the bar in what looked like a miniature glass coffin was a Marlene Dietrich doll wearing a tuxedo. Rainbow flags hung from every available spot, plastic-covered colored lights looped over the bar and windows, and the walls sported paintings depicting badly proportioned gymnasts.

Given that I had been unable to fight my way into any other bar in Greenwich Village, I overcame my instinct to bolt and settled into a corner with a beer. The upstairs was a piano bar; supposedly a dance floor lurked downstairs for the evening crowd, but I never made a return visit to see it open, instead limiting my visits to the afternoon hours.

Mercifully, no one touched either of the two baby grands during my first visit. However, some friends and I stopped by the next afternoon for a little cool air and liquid refreshment after fighting our way through the crowds of queers making the pilgrimage to the Stonewall bar. Although I had prayed I wouldn't hear it during my stay, some twisted queen began tickling the keys and warbling "New York, New York." Worse, a mob of southerners began belting out "Dixie." Hearing the theme song of the Old South, I burst into a short impromptu version of "*Deutschland Uber Alles*." Shortly after, I was persuaded to move on to another establishment.

The Village itself was so mindbogglingly crowded that I didn't manage to check out any other neighborhood bars or clubs. Each one had a block-long waiting line by sunset. I realized I would have to find a different neighborhood if I wanted to have a cocktail during my evening explorations.

One thing that comes up in every gushing conversation about New York (and usually while complaining about Washington, DC, in the same breath) is the abundance of super-clubs: the Roxy, Limelight, etc., etc. Wanting to experience the full effect of New York nightlife, I made a Wednesday night trip to USA, just off Broadway and Times Square.

Of course, as was the case with every club in the city, a special event for Stonewall 25 was underway, in this case the Bang-A-Gong Drag-A-Thon, billed as a "Salute to Wigstock Hosted by the Lady Bunny." All I know is that I got ripped for twenty bucks at the door.

Don't get me wrong—the interior is amazing. I wandered all over the damn place and I still think I missed some of the hidden rooms. Everywhere I turned there was a lounge, a mini dance floor, a roof-top deck, or a peep-show booth. A friend of mine discovered that the peep shows cost twenty-five cents and played for approximately fifteen seconds; however, no one would try to kick you out if the movie wasn't running, making the booths a nice place to visit with a new friend. The hundred-foot twisting slide called the K-hole and a huge neon sign above the dance floor flashing "*Drugs*" gave the impression that illegal substances may be necessary to fully appreciate the ambiance.

The only real fun I had at USA was following a gaggle of drag queens (dressed as West Hollywood cheerleaders, no less) from the roof deck down to the main dance floor. In a tiny hallway going down, one of them almost decapitated herself when her wood-reinforced wig caught hold of the ceiling. I still have bite marks in my tongue from trying not to laugh—these girls would have torn me limb from limb.

All in all, I didn't find myself entranced (perhaps I should have scraped up the money to follow the advice of the neon signs), and I left early. Of course, I missed the surprise appearance of Wesley Snipes and Patrick Swayze as they researched their roles as drag queens in *To Wong Foo, Thanks for Everything, Julie Newmar.*

What a shame.

When I told a friend that I had stopped by a gay sports bar, he instantly said, "Oh, you were in Chelsea."

If my reading of the neighborhood and various gay guides to Manhattan are correct, Chelsea has become the new living area for the slightly-higher-than-average income crowd (the much-higher-than-average income crowd apparently lives further north). Two of the Chelsea bars I visited, the sports-centered Champs and the self-touted "most popular bar in New York," Splash, seemed to fit a particular mode: young, professional gay heaven.

I had the good fortune of stumbling into Champs on opening night for a two-hour open bar, including free hot dogs and chicken wings. For what's basically a two-room cruise bar (or stand and model bar, depending on your perspective), I was amazed by the amount of money they had poured into it. Banks of video screens displayed ancient sailors-on-leave pornography, while the crowd mingled on the basketball court floor. The miniature boxing ring in one corner and the marble in the bathroom reminded me how little effort it takes for a hometown club to please me. Hell, I'm usually happy when a bar provides a toilet that flushes after every other use.

Of course, what bar in New York would be complete without go-go boys? Champs had one dancing in boxing gloves and a jock strap. Splash features hot boys taking showers then dancing out across the bar. And every club claimed to have "the hottest go-go boys." You can't hop two bars in Manhattan without running into a semi-naked man showcasing his wares from a block or bar. And dancing boys are nearly as ubiquitous as back rooms.

Speaking of back rooms, not that I would know anything specific, I managed to visit a number of places with posted signs warning "No Lips Below the Hips." Some of the back rooms in New York take this warning very seriously. According to my "sources," the rumpus rooms in some major clubs employ monitors with flyswatters to stop action that gets a tad too intense.

I most enjoyed the back room at the Crowbar in the East Village, a tiny, two-room place about the size of an efficiency with a walk-in closet. The elaborate sound system consisted of two Peavey speakers on opposite sides of the room; roughly the same technology on display at my college fraternity, but Crowbar plays better music. Posted at the entrance to the back room were two signs: *"No Wallets"* and, below that, *"Watch Your Wallet."* I couldn't figure out if the first sign was to scare away the pickpockets and the second to warn the customers, or if the management was just confused. Either sign can be taken as fair warning, since the Crowbar is so dark and crowded you never know who or what you'll grab next.

Along with my friends Sam and Ryan, I decided to give one of the notorious "private" sex clubs a shot. After much confusion determining the location of one (why are these places always near a major body of water?), we hailed a cab. Unfortunately, the driver decided it would be more efficient to take a rowdy group of queers to the nearest gay bar, which delayed our arrival by thirty minutes or so. When we finally reached our sexual destination, we spotted an enormous sign on the door announcing *"We Do Not Serve Alcohol."*

"I don't think so," Sam said, quickly shoveling us into the next available taxi. Lucky for him, the bars stay open until 4:00 AM.

Like the March on Washington, Stonewall 25 attracted a phenomenal number of promoters, political organizations, and others out to raise funds or, in many cases, just make a buck. Flipping through any gay publication in the weeks before the event, I found so many parties with fifty-dollar-and-up admission I nearly had a stroke. Being genetically averse to spending more than ten bucks to enter a decorated warehouse or warship, I avoided these "parties."

Okay, okay. The truth is, I was too broke to get in and I wasn't close enough friends with anyone who

could give me a free ticket. Who the hell can afford to go
to these things anyway? Between admission, cocktails,
and other omnipresent party favors that keep the spirit
going until seven in the morning, the total bill can
easily top five hundred dollars (more if you're trying
to impress a potential trick). I have a sneaky suspicion
that no one actually pays for or attends these parties;
it's actually a secret cabal that meets this way to develop
the "Gay Agenda" and figure out new ways to convert
heterosexuals.

Just a thought.

After seeing the predictably small attendance figures for
the march released by the police, I had to wonder why
queers always have to march on Sunday. Anyone in New
York for Stonewall knew there were more people in town
than we had at the March on Washington. So where
was everybody? They were in bed recovering from three
days of special receptions, parties, and after-hours parties.
Trust me, I know.

So, a bit of free advice for future organizers of
major queer events: Acknowledge the fact that when
gays and lesbians overrun a major city for a political
demonstration, they expect to have some serious fun.
With this in mind, schedule the march for Saturday
morning, before anyone has time to develop a serious
buzz. The march will then be filled with sunny, fresh-

faced queers ready to stand up for their rights. Then, when the rally ends at around two, everyone will have time to change before the four o'clock tea dance.

God knows partying is important. But so is being counted.

Gender Neutral

One crowded night in a local boy bar, I attempted to bypass the line for a urinal by ducking into the women's room. When I entered, two women at the mirror turned and stared at me in surprise.

"I thought this was the ladies' room," said the one with the bigger hair.

"That's what I thought," I replied. "Wanna do a quick check?" Not sure whose nether regions would be inspected for purity, they quickly exited, leaving me to take care of my business in relative peace.

Perhaps it's just me, but I don't see any problem with designating all queer-bar bathrooms as unisex. If we rightly believe that queer military men can bunk with straights in submarines without any problem, why don't more women believe they can share their bathrooms with men who aren't sexually attracted to them? It's not as if we're going in there to drill a peephole in the wall (those guys are too busy drilling holes between the stalls in the men's rooms of downtown department stores).

Although I rarely set foot in a straight bar these days, making me a de facto queer separatist, I do know of the enormous lines that always form outside the women's room. Why the women in these lines don't start a violent revolution, I don't know. If I were a girl, I'd be cutting in front of the boys' line in a heartbeat.

Perhaps it's a hetero thing. I've noticed that straight men would rather have a testicle pierced with a hot iron than be seen entering a room marked "ladies," regardless of how much beer has gone straight to their bladder.

Face the facts: Women's rooms are nicer than men's rooms. They're cleaner, they're bigger, and they're oh-so-much-more private. Women don't have to deal with those damn urinals that not only put you on display but hold all manner of disgusting things that can't be flushed away. On top of that, splashes resulting from poor urinal design are responsible for some of the most embarrassing wet spots known to man.

And not the least of the benefits of the ladies' room is the much-larger mirror to review the goods before going back out on the hunt.

Think about it—have you ever seen a women's room with men's-dormitory-style stalls, the ones with no doors that put all private functions on display to the world? Of course not. One of the few good things about women being considered "demure" is the privacy that comes with it.

If you should find yourself in the above situation, with a group of belligerent women upset with your presence in their peaceful sanctuary, try one of the following excuses.

"I'm sorry, but I'm pee shy." (Make sure to bend over slightly while grimacing.)

"I just want to check if I'm still bleeding." (Proceed to walk bowlegged to the stall.)

If you happen to be with a friend, you need an excuse for both of you.

"He has to come with me. He has the key."

"I need help to change my Depends. By the way, do they sell sanitary napkins in here?"

That should guarantee you all the privacy you'll ever need.

Housing Policy

One of the most difficult decisions you can make in your life is whether to have a roommate. And if the best housing you can currently afford would best be termed a hovel, the decision may be whether to have multiple roommates.

While roommates can make one's life financially easier, they can also make one's life a living hell. This is particularly true when your roommates bring home a successive string of boyfriends who are apparently on work-release from the local asylum.

In past dealings with group housing situations, I've found that the best roommates are women. An instant plus is that they most likely will not follow you around everywhere you go (as some queer roommates are wont to do), and therefore will not be present every time you make a fool of yourself in the bar trying to pick up some cute twenty-one-year-old with a "hello gay" buzz cut.

Female roommates have served various functions in my past households, beginning with detective. One morning they found a leather jacket hanging from the banister and quickly began to piece together my previous evening of fun. While I slept, blissfully unaware of what other creature(s) might be sharing my mattress, they quickly rifled through the pockets and found the prize piece of evidence: a bottle of Oxy 10.

They also have served as harbingers of doom. One temporary boyfriend of mine had a propensity to make sudden visits to our happy home, intruding on our regular group gathering to watch *Twin Peaks*. While we were trying to follow the travails of the Log Lady, he would attempt to regale us with stories of New York.

"I was at a party in New York one time," he would say to the backs of our heads. "I ran into William Hurt and Marlee Matlin. And let me tell you, she was so drunk she was slurring her sign!"

I calmly watched my roommates as their eyes grew wider and their jaws clenched tighter. Shortly after, I noticed their fingers, which were keeping a tally of the number of times the soon-to-be ex-boyfriend said "New York." I quickly managed to feign complete exhaustion, knowing that if I didn't get this irritant out of the room, my roommates would eventually rip out his tongue.

Although my roommates would seem to have been complete angels, some problems have arisen. Once, after arriving home from a hard day at work, I found one roommate waiting to talk to me about the rent. Needing to relax, I asked her to wait and retired to my bedroom for a few moments with my favorite magazine.

As I was turning to page 38 ("Shower Nymph"), she came into my room, demanding to have the discussion there and then. I managed to drive her out of the room with a pillow, but by then the moment had been lost.

So, if you are casting about for roommates, remember: any roommate can be a good roommate, as long as your bedroom door locks.

Multiple Maniacs

O ne of the more vexing problems of etiquette is
how to conduct yourself when having anonymous
group or back-room sex (a much more important problem,
I believe, than remembering how to use a fish knife). So,
once again, I've developed some ground rules to help the
social lubrication.

Don't expect pillow-talk.

One time, after only a brief assignation, my partner
suddenly became attached to my hip as I waited for my
friend to find his way out of the maze in the back. In an
attempt to extricate myself, I told him I had to leave.

"Can't you just sit here and cuddle for a few minutes?" he
asked, with large Bambi eyes. My only option was to run for
the front door and pray for a waiting cab, leaving my friend
to his own devices. (Bonus tip: never go to a sex club or party
with a friend who is unable to get home on his own.)

Remember that the point of anonymous sex is the
anonymity. Finding a private space with your temporary

84

partner is okay, but if you force your phone number on him afterward, don't expect a phone call anytime soon (unless you're extraordinarily talented).

If you want to cuddle, stay home with your boyfriend.

Do be friendly.

You don't have to strike up a conversation with everyone you see, but you should smile on occasion to keep the atmosphere festive. Be sure to say a quiet "Hi" if you see anyone you know. If you see a closeted celebrity or congressman, be sure to call out his name loudly across the sea of gyrating bodies.

Watch those hands.

Regardless of how sexy you think you are, not everyone is going to agree. Therefore, your groping little hand may not be welcome by the couple whose action you're trying to horn in on.

Once, when I made the mistake of closing my eyes while enjoying a particular carnal act, I slowly became aware that my partner had apparently grown six extra arms. I opened my eyes to discover that I had become the center of a bizarre mating ritual of the trolls.

A key phrase to remember is, "No means no." A slap on the hand or other offending appendage also means "no." If you find yourself in the center of an unwanted group grope that refuses to disperse, just say loudly, "Don't make me slap your hand again, or I'll pull this condom over your head and laugh when you turn blue."

Of course, there are times when touching is unavoidable. When moving through a crowded back room, for example, you often can't avoid making hand contact with random, naked, sweating butts no matter where you turn. Just make sure you don't lose your hand in one of them.

Don't go looking for love.
You'll only be disappointed.

Three-Way Etiquette

One of the great blessings of queer life, as well as one of the reasons straight men are so jealous of us, is our sexual creativity. After all, how often do you hear hetero couples going on about their latest three-way?

While many queer couples consider three-ways more fun than a barrel of monkeys chewing on Pop Rocks, most of them neglect the careful planning and execution of the events that guarantee a good time will be had by all (and a divorce will not occur the next day).

So, in the interest of smoother social interaction, here are some etiquette tips for those couples hunting down "an extra" for the evening. I must mention that these tips deal only with three-ways. Situations involving four or more people, while increasing the options for pleasure, also create a myriad of potentially sticky situations that would warrant an entire book of their own.

Etiquette Tip Number One: Do not be rude when turning down your partner's choice.

There is no good reason to destroy someone's self-esteem by yelling, "What are you thinking? You don't expect me to go home with that?" A quiet "No way in hell" whispered in your partner's ear will suffice.

If you and your partner are each actively searching for a third, you can be assured that both of you will find your perfect man (aside from each other, of course). In this event, either flip a coin to decide the lucky winner or split up for the evening. If you attempt a four-way, you will end up with two separate couples fighting for bed space.

Etiquette Tip Number Two: Be active.

Pardon the pun, but if you act like a third wheel you'll just bring everybody down. If necessary, close your eyes and pretend Keanu Reeves stopped by for a visit. *

If you find that the whole situation is still unappetizing, assume an authoritarian role and begin to direct the action. It can be an enormous turn-on to order your partner to do all the things he refuses to do with you alone—it would be rude of him to refuse in front of company. If your partner has recently forgotten your birthday or anniversary, be sure to order him to contort into the shape of a pretzel.

Etiquette Tip Number Three: Be prepared.

When you and your partner are both in the mood to be passive, you most likely will be looking for a top. However, any three-way that comes together in a nightclub around 4:00 AM will run the risk of becoming a battle of

---

*   *Keanu Reeves?* you're thinking. *That's even more dated than a shoe-sized cell phone.* Hey, it was the nineties. Like a pizza date with Bill Clinton, it seemed like a good idea at the time.

the bottoms. Be sure to have a cock ring handy to help someone get it up.

If the extra constriction of blood flow doesn't do the trick, break out a selection of dildos and try to be creative. Perhaps someday a wise entrepreneur will save you the trouble and market a triple-headed dildo for just such an occasion.

Etiquette Tip Number Four: Do not bring in ex-boyfriends.

The only exception to this rule is when you're trying to get back at your current boyfriend. In that case, be sure not to mention your ex-lover's true identity until the next morning over breakfast.

Dancing Days

Perhaps because my first visit to a gay bar in Washington was a trip upstairs at Rascals, I have developed over the years a certain affinity for watching go-go boys dance naked (which I pronounced "nekkid" during my early years in the city).

Yes, it was for this that I left home.

It was also on that first trip to Rascals that I met two particular types of personalities, in this case combined in the same dancer: an exhibitionist (he could tie himself in a knot, if you know what I mean) and a pathological liar (he regaled us with tales of the hot tub party behind the stage).

Since then, my trips to the dick bar have become more confident and frequent. Instead of sitting at the bar drooling shyly into my cocktail, I became quite the social butterfly when faced with a dancer's pendulosities dangling near my face. In fact, I found that many of the dancers would come to me to have their egos stroked and thereby increase their tips. I'm not sure if this is because of my looks or because of my soft and supple hands that have been untouched by the toil of hard labor.

Being the curious soul that I am, I wanted to know what it would be like on top of the bar, serving instead of being served. Naturally, I stumbled into one bar (now the site of a parking lot) after a number of cocktails and asked the manager if my friend and I could make a go of it.

Unbeknownst to me at the time, the managers and bartenders had a policy of attempting to get cute customers onto the stage. The key tool of this policy was free banana-flavored shooters. The lesson in this is to wait for a free cocktail before you strip. Consider it your first tip.

The manager put us on the back stage. My friend and I began undressing while attempting to keep a drunken rhythm to the blasting, generic disco. Many dancers I had seen used the brass pole for various acrobatic and erotic stunts—I used it to keep from falling on my nekkid ass.

My friend made it down to his underwear before he realized what he was doing and quickly jumped off the stage. Blessed with an inability to feel embarrassment, I blithely continued my routine.

My immediate concern was an erection to keep the audience's attention. The management had supplied a bottle of hand lotion for just this purpose and within a few minutes I managed to get to full mast. The crowd in the back area doubled from three to six. Whether this was a comment on my endowment or their boredom with the other dancers, I'm not sure.

Although I had embarked on this sordid little journey just to find out what it felt like, the scratching of bills being shoved into my socks alerted me to the fact I had begun making money. When I finished my set, I found that I had made about forty bucks in thirty minutes.

With that hourly rate, I was tempted to quit my job and stay there forever. I just couldn't figure out how to fit it on my resume.

Speed Racer

We've all heard of ways to make sex more exciting, and have even come up with some of our own: latex toys, fur-padded cuffs, fresh produce, nylon stockings ... well, you get my point.

Even with all these options before me, it hasn't always done the trick. In fact, only one thing has consistently produced the desired enhancement to my sexual pleasure: the constraints of time. After all, what would an assignation be if it were not brief?

I learned this interesting fact of life at an early age. While it seems all my adult queer friends were humping each other from elementary school onward, I was left to my own devices in rural America with nothing but the Sears catalog. Needless to say, I got to be quite inventive.

I rode the bus to school (the big bus, of course). Since children were always being scared out of their wits by bus safety films, my bus had to drive a mile past my house, turn around, and come back so no kid would have to cross the road. I know it sounds laborious, but trust me, you haven't seen maniacs drive until you've been to the hills of Kentucky.

Anyway ...

The bus always made its first pass at 7:25 AM. It took a total of five minutes for it to return to find my sister and me on the porch. Of course, every time I saw the bus I was overcome with a sudden urge to run to the bathroom and "relieve" myself.

I knew my time was limited (who wants to be embarrassed by having the bus driver lay on the horn outside their house?) so I did my business as quickly as possible. I didn't even need the magazine with the full-page Jim Palmer Jockey advertisement, my own pre-pubescent porno. Just unzip and go.

Sometimes I would even wait for a few minutes before starting, just to make the whole thing more challenging and dangerous. I'm not sure, but I think my therapist would see definite signs of obsessive-compulsive disorder in my young actions. If only my parents had known of Ritalin.

From all the public and semi-public sex that goes on in DC (not that I would know anything about it), I'm convinced that I'm not the only one with a time fixation. When a cute couple leaves the bar for a quick romp in the car, why is it fun? Because of the danger of getting caught?

Partly. But even more, it's fun because you don't have much time. After all, if you're having sex in a car on a public street, it's not a matter of *if* you will get caught, but *when*. It's all about finishing before you're found. Sort of like when you rush to finish and get back to your boyfriend before he figures out that you didn't go to the cash machine. Or finishing with someone else's boyfriend before that special someone begins banging on the stall door.

The moral of the story, if morals can be said to have any part in it, is that sex under the gun is the most fun. After all, it's the thrill that counts.

The Ex of My Boyfriend Is My Ex

Everyone knows that relationships come laden with emotional baggage: fear of commitment, fear of intimacy, inability to keep an apartment clean, and so on. Most of these can be dealt with effectively by a few hours of horrendously expensive therapy (perhaps with a prescription thrown in for good measure), resulting in a healthy, stable relationship.

However, there is one piece of baggage that no therapist or pharmaceutical can hide: a lover's ex-boyfriend. With the current quest for mental stability, inner peace, or other New Age state-of-mind, far too many men are breaking up with the promise to "just be friends."

And, surprisingly enough, they're keeping their promise.

So for all of you who have been forced to deal with your partner's over-friendly ex and the emotional baggage he brings (such as feelings of inadequacy, jealousy, and homicide), I've put together some suggestions for dealing with some of the more common situations.

Running Into the Ex at a Bar.

If you're with your boyfriend, try to be nice and buy the ex a drink. Make the drink particularly colorful in case you have to accidentally spill it on him during the course of the evening.

If you're alone when you encounter the ex, be nice and buy him a drink. Invite him to the bathroom to attempt a fast and dirty seduction. If he rejects you, accidentally spill your drink on him.

Taking His Phone Calls.

Answering machines and voice mail were invented for screening calls and erasing messages from people you don't want to speak to (or your boyfriend to hear from). Just make sure you check it before your boyfriend does.

At Your Dinner Party.

Most likely the ex will bring his current boyfriend, so you won't be alone in your seething. Still, it is imperative that you keep a cheerful face as you try to decide who your boyfriend is paying more attention to—you or the ex. You're in real trouble if he pays more attention to the ex's boyfriend.

As an emergency measure in case of a disaster, be ready to serve a salmon mousse with a touch of botulism. You can always start with a clean slate tomorrow.

At Cocktail Parties.

This calls for even more politeness than a bar, as more of the people watching you freak out will know your name. Etiquette demands that you stand there with a smile on your face while the ex regales everyone with the story of the summer he spent in Greece with your boyfriend.

Fortunately, etiquette has given us queers a weapon: repeated viewings of *All About Eve* and *The Women* will do wonders for your biting sarcasm. Be sure to make every evil (yet polite) word count.

With Your Boyfriend in a Public Place.

Few things are worse than stumbling upon your boyfriend having dinner and/or drinks with his ex. If things are above-board, they will ask you to join them. If they don't offer, you must insist.

With Your Boyfriend in a Private Place.

If it's your living room, there may still be hope. If it's your bedroom, start packing things immediately.

Your new ex-boyfriend's things, of course.

Killing Time

For many years, the prospect of going out to a bar by myself terrified me. Standing alone, anxiously gripping a cocktail, while waiting for some non-psychopath to begin a stimulating conversation was too much like a stomach-wrenching trip to the high-school cafeteria where I ate my lunch alone at an enormous table, far away from the marauding rednecks by the patio door (where smoking and chewing tobacco were allowed). I'm sure everyone has been through this humiliating experience. If not, it's a geek thing, you wouldn't understand.

Nowadays, I understand the joy and freedom of occasionally venturing out alone. After all, who needs competition from a friend for that cute twenty-two-year-old who just moved here from Kansas? My newfound ability to comfortably enter a bar without companionship stems from the various techniques I've developed for distracting myself from my solitude.

First of all, pinball machines are a blessing for those out alone, particularly if they're located in a smaller section of the bar, away from the main cruising section. Even I need a break sometimes. However, even though pinball can make the hours speed by, you're not going to attract any cute young guys by wildly slapping flippers.

I also kill time with the classic poor-man's bar game, *How Long Can One Beer Last?* The rules are simple: constantly tell yourself that you won't take a sip until the next video is over. Before you know it, the clock will read 1:00 AM and your beer will taste like warm spit. As an added advantage to stretching out your drink, you probably won't find yourself later in the evening throwing up on Mr. Right's new loafers.

If you master this game, increase the difficulty by attempting to light a cigarette with slightly soggy matches without setting down your bottle. When you can perform this feat, there's not much left in life for you to do other than become a surgeon.

Other times I occupy myself by counting the number of times the DJ plays certain videos, thereby acquainting myself with the sometimes excruciatingly bad musical taste of our community. In fact, I've decided that if I'm subjected one more time to Elton John and RuPaul exhorting each other "Don't Go Breaking My Heart," I'll begin throwing beer bottles at the DJ booth.

When all else fails, I've found it useful to retreat to the classic lonely-man-in-a-bar pose: stand in the corner looking forlorn and hope someone takes pity on you.

This works best when you display your best Disney-esque, puppy-dog eyes. But don't overdo it; people may ask if you know where they can get some good "stuff."

Regardless how bored or lonely you may feel, never annoy the bartenders. Yes, it is part of their job to cheerfully chit-chat with the customers as they sling the cocktails. But no, they do not want to hear all the details of your Aunt Millie's hip-replacement surgery.

Come to think of it, maybe it would be better if I just went out with friends. After all, a little competition never hurt anyone.

Blank Moments

Show me a gay man who hasn't run into a fellow queer in a bar and realized he's forgotten the man's name, and I'll show you a gay man who lives in a town once featured on *Hee Haw* (Population 347! Saaaaaa-lute!).

Every time I run into this embarrassing situation, my mind immediately attempts to make the situation even worse by asking, "Have I slept with him?" It's one thing to have a reputation as a floozy—it's quite another to have the reputation proven by running out of space in your mental Rolodex.

The embarrassment isn't that big of a deal when I've only spotted the familiar-looking man from across the bar. In fact, it's comforting to know that, if he is indeed a former trick, his mental gears are as likely to be grinding away to remember my name as mine are his.

Unless, of course, I've never actually met the man, much less shared an evening (or hour) of carnal pleasure. In that case, while I'm desperately trying to place his face with a fleeting moment from my past, he's looking for the nearest phone to call the police and file a stalking complaint.

Far worse are those moments when a stranger approaches me in a bar, kisses my cheek, and begins talking as if he's been my best friend since kindergarten. In another unfortunate quirk of Mother Nature's order of the universe, my first instinct is not to interrupt him with the direct and effective question, "I'm sorry, but who exactly might you be?"

Instead, in the interest of being polite, I always start the conversational equivalent of Twenty Questions (The Search for the Missing Identity Edition):

"So, how's the job going?"

"Pretty good, can't complain. Yours?"

"Fine, fine." *Pause for a long drink from my beer bottle.* "Still living in the same place?"

"Yeah."

"That's good." *Over-elaborate search for cigarettes to buy a few more precious seconds.* "So ... haven't seen you out lately."

"Nope, haven't been out much."

"Yeah, I know what you mean." *Set my suddenly empty bottle down on the nearest available flat surface.* "Gotta go to the bathroom. Be right back." *Run for the nearest exit.*

I've always found it much easier to deal with the situation when I have some friends nearby to save me from the rampant vacuousness of the conversation. Most of my friends happen to be well-trained and will jump in after an appropriate amount of time and introduce themselves (usually around three minutes, though if the conversation gets particularly silly it can be around thirty seconds).

After the names have been exchanged, all I have to do is laugh heartily and say, "I'm so sorry, I thought you two knew each other. Isn't that funny?"

Friends who are tuned in to the situation will then ask something along the lines of, "So, how do you know my friend?" Just hope they don't hit the unintended jackpot: "We got arrested together one night in P Street Beach." Of course, that pretty much clears up the sex question.

Sidewalk Cruising

O ne of the more enjoyable aspects of life in the city is sidewalk socializing. As well as being the most convenient form of transportation for those of us too poor to afford a Yugo, sidewalks are the best place to carry on conversations with people I know but wouldn't invite over for dinner. I love to take visiting friends through my queer little neighborhood, saying "hi" to every other person I see. The fact that I can't remember anyone's name is beside the point.

Many people (i.e., friends of mine) use the sidewalk to make new, temporary friends. Personally, I haven't had the best of luck forming these types of friendships while in the outdoors, not counting public places with an abundance of bushes and trees. And while the sight of me walking home from an after-hours party can cause small children to burst into tears, some queer boys can't walk home at seven o'clock in the morning without being invited inside for a brief tryst by some guy walking his poodle.

I have the wrong attitude for street pickups. Since I can't go outside with the outline of a cigarette pack in my pocket without being accosted by every nicotine-addicted street person in a three-mile radius, I've found myself in the habit of saying "no" to anyone in my path. Still, some people have seen beyond my nasty exterior and attempted to reach out to me.

One evening around midnight, as I walked home from a friend's apartment, a white Hyundai pulled up to the curb. The driver had rolled down the passenger-side window before the car completely stopped.

The tiny bit of country boy still living inside me blithely assumed the man wanted to ask for directions, and I leaned down to offer my assistance. The city boy inside me forced me to stay a respectable distance from the car, the better to make a run for it if the guy turned out to be the president of the John Wayne Gacy fan club (motto: "Clowns Are Your Friends.")

"Do you know where the St. Francis School is?" he asked.

"Hmmmm …" I said, looking casually up and down the street. Reasonably sure that no school would have continuing education classes scheduled at that particular time, I came to the rational conclusion that I might need a little more distance between me and the Hyundai.

"Sorry, I don't know where that is," I said, offering an apologetic smile and shrug as I backed away.

The man leaned closer to the window. "Can I suck your dick then?"

"Nope, sorry." For lack of any other gesture appropriate to the situation, I offered the same apologetic shrug (Miss Manners, where are you when I need you?). I then bit my tongue to avoid laughing and quickly resumed my walk home.

While the man's request took me by surprise, it certainly was more polite than the other request I recently received at gunpoint while on my way to lunch: "Give it up or I'll blow your fucking head off." I chose what was behind curtain number one and handed over my personal effects; I was hungry and I wanted to get to McDonald's.

So I say "yes" to a mugging and "no" to a blow job. Where are my priorities?

Twenty-Four Seven

I f it weren't for 7-Eleven, you wouldn't be reading this.
I awoke this morning thinking I would quickly dash
off a few hundred words about sex, parties, or some other
important aspect of the universe. Instead, I found myself
staring into a refrigerator that lacked the most important
ingredient of my work: coffee.

Or, more specifically, caffeine. So I found myself
once again in the early hours running to my friends for
help. Where would the world be without the friendly,
neighborhood 7-Eleven? Bereft of burritos, for one
thing.

In college, I would make midnight runs from the
fraternity house for another round of munchies before
re-packing the bong; after smoking that, I would run
back for chili dogs. It was during this time I discovered
that 7-Eleven was the place to eat when the check from
my parents was late. Just buy a hot dog, use the lid of
the container as a bowl, and pump away on the chili

dispenser. It was more economical than Wendy's, and I could surreptitiously go back for seconds.

Now that I've become a more responsible queer, I find myself plundering the mixers section for an impromptu morning soiree after the bar finally kicks us out. The best thing is that the twenty-four-hour piece-of-heaven always has other items required to sustain your reputation as an after-hours host: Twinkies, Doritos, and Ding-Dongs (which have been renamed King Dons, but I prefer the Jeff Stryker imagery of the original name).

A nearby 7-Eleven is better than having a boyfriend. The employees serve you. They take care of you. They help you out the door when you pass out in front of the auto supplies shelf.

I've come to think of the entire 7-Eleven shopping experience as a visit with family. After all, I'm met outside the door by neighborhood residents who warmly greet me with a smile (except my grandmother never asks me if I can spare any change when I leave, although she has mentioned the practice of tithing on occasion).

The cashiers immediately pull down my brand of cigarettes before I have a chance to ask. If I tell them I don't need any cigs, they become concerned with my health. "It is a good thing that you are quitting. Are you sure you do not need any?"

They even let me play with the electric *Mighty Morphin' Power Rangers* suckers sitting by the register.

One of my friends has an even closer relationship with the 7-Eleven family. He has a habit of stumbling into the store shortly after last call and raiding the stock of burritos. As he shoves five of the extra-hot beef-n-beans into the microwave, the staff keeps a tally. They cheerfully wave good-bye as he wanders out of the store with hot burritos sticking out of his pockets. And, just like the father who gently reminds you about the money you borrowed, they present him with his complete bill the next day.

These are the stories that warm my heart. I would tell more of them, but I have to go get a refill.

Very Inane People

How often have you heard someone refer to Washington's only product being legislation? Well, no matter how many times it's been said, it's still wrong.

Washington's biggest product is self-importance.

No, I'm not going off on another anti-A-lister rant, although I believe A-listers could add to their beloved family fortunes (whether real or imagined) by skimming the excess ego off their fake-and-bake hides, bottling the resulting ooze, and marketing it in the Midwest as the most life-changing product since Didi-7. They are part of the problem, yes, but an even more frightening creature lurks among us ....

The A-lister wannabe.

You know the type: thirty seconds into any conversation, he's complaining about all the stress he's under in his high-level position with some agency, the name of which you didn't quite catch, and conspicuously dropping money machine receipts with astronomically high balances. Odds are he picked up the receipts as he withdrew his last ten dollars before heading to the bar. Manage to surprise him at work, and you'll probably find him wearing a paper hat and apron.

But adversity certainly doesn't keep the A-lister wannabe from inflating his station in life. When scandals hit the front page of the *Post*, he's the one who says, "So-and-so, my friend in the White House, says ...." Come on. In the Clinton era, with a town full of government bureaucrats running around feeling our pain, what self-respecting queer *doesn't* have a contact in the Administration?

No matter how annoying it is, the mindset is pervasive. Think of the New York-style fake velvet ropes that some clubs adopt in an attempt to make the average club-goer feel inadequate. Or the fake lines of people waiting to get in the door to some clubs, which I can only assume are supposed to make you believe the club is actually crowded this week.

And don't forget those stupid VIP lounges that proliferated in nightclubs for a while, and are still in fashion at many of the overpriced black-tie fundraisers (I would think that any charitable organization that can charge more than $150 for a ticket and keep a straight face would consider anyone who bothered to come a very important person).

I've never quite figured out who's sillier, those who thought they were important because they got in or those who thought they were important because they controlled the gate. After all, what's the big deal about VIP rooms if you still have to pay for drinks? You can get better service on a downward-bound USAir flight.

Proximity to politicians must be at the root of all this. We've all been forced to deal with the self-important queer who does have a job. "The fate of the inverse-index of income of international raw papaya surpluses rests only my shoulders, and mine alone!"

Ooops! I gotta go. My friend at the Old Executive Office building just paged me. Now he *really* knows what's going on.

Trick or Treat

'Tis the season to pretend you're someone you're not and beg from your neighbors: Halloween, the official queer holiday. In a public-service effort to avert a flood of misguided queens attempting drag for the first time, I've put together a handy list of truly scary costumes for your trick-or-treating rounds. For your safety, none of the following disguises require you to break your ankle in bad-fitting high heels or buy a set of falsies.

The Closeted Professional.

A nondescript, charcoal-gray suit will work wonders. For the finishing touch, add a colorful, expensive tie so anyone who's "family" will get the message. To add new levels of terror, carry around the picture that came with your wallet so you'll have proof when joining the office guy-talk about girlfriends.

If someone refuses to give you candy, offer to write a check to their favorite gay charity. After you reap your reward, report your checkbook stolen and cancel the check.

The Activist Fascist.

A leather or jean jacket festooned with politically-correct buttons will tell every man you meet what's wrong with his life. While trick-or-treating, loudly demand your fair share of the booty. Ask why the kids dressed as *Mighty Morphin' Power Rangers* are getting all the damn Sweet Tarts.

If anyone refuses to honor your demands, chain yourself to the door and begin chanting "I'm here, I'm queer, and I want Milk Duds." If they give you candy, do it anyway.

Executive Director of a Gay Organization.

Similar to the closeted professional, but the suit should have a bit more flair. When you get a handful of candy thrown in your bag, hand your generous donor a lovely thank-you card. Then ask for more (think Oliver Twist). If they don't pony up, threaten to send them an invitation to every fundraiser scheduled for the next two years. If that doesn't work, give them a job.

The Ex-Gay.

Khakis, loafers, a pastel shirt, and a drool cup. For added emphasis, have a confused-looking, big-haired woman holding your hand. If a cute man gives you candy, invite him to a party later that night at your residence, the men's live-in program. If someone cute doesn't give you a treat, memorize his address so you can begin your stalking routine.

The Sullen Teenager.

Pick up a Metallica or O.J. Simpson t-shirt from a street vendor. Run around your neighborhood carrying an extra-large Hefty trash bag. Remember, people aren't frightened of cherry bombs anymore. They are, however, frightened of a Glock semi-automatic with a full clip.

A Vampire.

Wear a Versace outfit (preferably one stolen from a trick in New York or Miami), and only go trick-or-treating in the best neighborhoods. After you get the treats, ask to use the phone so you can check on your ailing mother. While the host is distracted, swipe the rest of the candy and disappear.

A Witch.

Dress like your ex-boyfriend. After you get the candy say, "I love you." Then walk away and never speak to him again.

A Bitch.

Go as yourself.

Bar Talk

I s it just me, or is inane chatter a universal truth of gay bars?

When talking to someone you've known for years but never liked, inane conversation is the only polite option. Life would be more fun, though less civil, if you could throw sonic daggers: "I've heard that you make the cutest little squealing sound when you're getting plowed," or "Exactly how long was your jail term, anyway?"

But I'm usually too nice to blow off unwanted interlopers on my personal space with such verbal jabs, unless the annoying chatterer happens to be an ex-boyfriend. In that case, these attacks are allowed under the Geneva Convention.

Because of this, I had anticipated a recent business trip to New York as an opportunity for refreshing conversations with new people. Being the shy person that I am, I went to the nearest bar and planted myself against the wall. If there's anything I hate more than stupid bar talk, it's contributing to the problem with my own stupid opening lines ("Hi, I make a living writing about my sex life and it only takes fifty milligrams of medication a day to keep me from having a psychotic break right now. How about you?").

First up was a schoolteacher couple celebrating their tenth anniversary. Employing the "Can I bum a cigarette" routine, the educational couple soon had me roped into a history of their life together, including summer trips to Czechoslovakia.

"Once, two bears charged us while we were outside the hotel," one of them said.

"Yeah, yeah," the other chimed in. "I was scared to death, but he started clapping, and the bears ran up a tree."

Although I was fascinated to hear about Czechoslovakian bears that come equipped with Clappers, I realized the situation was only going to deteriorate and began looking for escape routes. When one of them said they usually found "thirds" for the evening, I bolted for the exit.

I then had a brief conversation with someone who claimed to be on the editorial staff of a major publishing house. He kept telling me how beautiful I was. Given his stated occupation, I would have preferred observations about my obvious natural talent. However, I decided not to attempt clinching my first book deal by sleeping my way up the ladder and excused myself to the bathroom.

I often wonder about the wisdom of that decision.

With the clock passing midnight, I decided to give up on the search for signs of intelligent conversation and dance to the music of my youth (A Flock of Seagulls and the Go-Gos, in case you were wondering). But before I could get from my bar stool to the dance floor, I was cornered by a young investment banker who told me he was just coming out of the closet.

"You probably don't like me because I want to make money," he said.

What's not to like about an avaricious queer, especially if he's out of the closet? Just because I've chosen a career path that will never push my savings account beyond four digits (including decimal places), why would I want to bring everyone else down?

Anyway, if someone out there doesn't make some serious bucks I'll never be able to find my own personal patron of the arts.

Hands Off

Some things in the world are simply annoying: bad hairpieces, inept clerks at McDonald's, alcohol-free beer, temporary loss of erection.

Some things in life, however, are far more disturbing. For example, if this city were really concerned about the sanity of its citizens, there would have been an initiative on Tuesday's ballot to outlaw bumming cigarettes on the street, a practice that has exceeded the bounds of "aggressive panhandling." I had grown accustomed to people quietly asking for a cancer stick and a quarter as I passed them on the way to the 7-Eleven. But nothing has prepared me for men yelling from the other side of the street, "Hey! Hey! Yeah, you! Gimme a cigarette!"

Should you refuse the request because you cannot afford to support every nicotine habit in the city (or because you don't smoke, which these combative types never seem to notice), be prepared for a harsher verbal attack than any you've received from an ex-boyfriend.

Of course, bumming a cigarette should remain legal within bars, where a little polite begging can be part of the courtship ritual. I, for one, would rather someone ask me for a smoke before saying, "I'd really like to fuck you." And I would *much* rather someone buy me a drink first.

There's direct and then there's *direct*, if you know what I mean.

As with all things, some individuals will abuse their freedom, claiming to have stopped smoking while sucking up three packs worth of other people's tobacco. This is the price we pay for living in a free society. But some prices are far too steep. There are certain acts that should be outlawed in bars, most importantly the crime of roving hands.

You know how it works. As you walk through a crowded bar, your butt suddenly becomes a magnet for fingers encased in thick gold rings, the owners of which can almost never be found. At times, I think I'm being cruised by Thing from *The Addams Family*.

And some people take the rude behavior even further. Not long ago, as I tried to squeeze a few games of pinball in between my Cape Cod refills, a fellow alum from college appeared. I did not consider him a welcome sight.

Before I could even get into multi-ball mode, he attached himself to me like a bad set of crabs, which would have been preferable since I have a standing prescription for that problem. Unfortunately, I don't know of any medicine short of Mace that could have gotten his hands off my body. I now have a much better understanding of why some cultures punish offenders by chopping off hands, a course of action we should perhaps consider.

Okay, I admit, that's a bit harsh for what can only be described as a subjective crime. There have been times when the owner of the offending hand on my butt turned out to be not so offensive. Or downright cute.

In that case, why worry about giving permission?

Size Queen

"There are two types of men in the world," the aphorism goes. "Size queens and liars."

Ever since junior high, I've been aware of the male fascination with phallic stature. The boys in the locker room were fascinated with the future size of their own penises. I, on the other hand, was entranced by the size of the wrestler who had been held back for two years.

This fascination with size is rampant in the gay community. Look at the titles of your favorite porno tapes: *Big Guns, Butt Busters, The Bigger the Better.* But have you ever seen a porno named *Small Wonders*? *

My own experience has found pros and cons for both the over- and under-endowed among us. My criteria for judgment rest on one standard: it's either bigger than mine or it's not. Scientific? No. Practical? Yes.

---

*   Of course, with the explosion of Internet porn tailored for the specific sexual tastes and fetishes of every known type, *Small Wonders* is now big business.

The French Test.

The primary advantage of a small penis can be boiled down to two words: deep throat. Even the most inexperienced novice can make like Linda Lovelace on a french fry. I love it because I don't have to hold my breath.

However, attempting to deep throat a penis larger than a ruler could make you a candidate for a segment of *Rescue 911,* particularly if you are cursed with oversized tonsils.

The Greek Test.

If you're a top, you can skip this part, as it does not apply to you in any way.

That's what I thought.

The small penis loses its advantage when it's attached to a top. First, you have to search for "snug-fitting" condoms (and you thought it was embarrassing to buy a pack of regular Trojans in high school). Second, it's frustrating to have your partner pop out every time he starts to hit a decent rhythm—when he tries to get back in, it takes him at least five tries to find the bull's-eye. It's like being examined by a farsighted proctologist.

As for the extra-large versions of manhood, don't worry about finding jumbo condoms—overly hung top men keep Trojan Magnums lying around the house like badges of honor. Instead, worry about what you're going to do when faced with such a large appendage. In terms of inches, it's really not that far from your anus to your esophagus.

Aesthetics count.

I've noticed that gay men want to believe that the bigger the penis, the more likely the owner is to be a top. When (not if) the prospective top turns out to be as big a bottom as everyone else, they just whisper to each other, "What a waste." This attitude completely overlooks the best thing about a big penis: it's fun just to look at it.

In the end (excuse the pun), I've found that average is best, particularly when faced with a penis so large it should have an escape hatch. Anyway, do I really want to get plowed by some guy whose penis looks like it's been doused in Miracle-Gro?

Or, more precisely, do I really want to sleep with anyone who's going to make me feel inadequate?

Ode to Porn

More than disco, pornography made me what I am today.

In Kentucky, small towns didn't have quite the selection of groceries and other supplies boasted by larger cities like Paducah, so long-haul shopping trips with Granny were the norm. Of course, I had ulterior motives for making the trip: whereas the only books available for purchase in Fredonia and the surrounding Caldwell County were located at Wal-Mart and a couple of rickety, plywood-fronted Christian outlets * , Paducah had actual bookstores I could roam for hours while Granny searched J.C. Penney's for the perfect bargain.

---

*   Fundamentalist Christian bookstores tended to pop up in storefronts where other businesses had recently failed. The number of stores in which one could buy the *Illustrated Children's Living Bible* and various Jesus trinkets served as an indicator of where the region currently stood in the boom-and-bust economic cycle.

During one pre-Christmas outing just before my seventeenth birthday, we made an unexpected detour through the farmer's market mini-mall. While she haggled in Piggly Wiggly, I explored a small magazine stand. And there I found what I had been waiting for:

Blueboy magazine.

It was hidden high up on the rack—I could see only the title and the top of a man's head, but I knew what it was. And the cover boy looked pretty hot. Who cared that the sign below it read, "You must be eighteen or older—no browsing." I took a deep breath and pulled the magazine off the rack.

The beautiful man on the cover hid his goods behind a pair of crossed skis. You can probably guess the caption: "Snowballs." I almost had a little accident before I even opened the thing. When I finally did, the threshold was crossed.

I didn't feel the guilt that struck when I stared at the semi-erect penises that occasionally graced the pages of *Hustler* or *Penthouse* that I had perused behind my dad's auto body shop. This man had posed naked for me, another man, to look at. The photographers and editors knew my desires, and they had taken the time to print a magazine just for me.

After a thorough examination of *Blueboy*, my shaking hands didn't have a chance to make it through *Inches*. An employee tapped me on the shoulder. "Are you eighteen?" Perhaps my high-school letter jacket tipped her off.

I suppose it may have been better had I also been exposed to the multitude of magazines available today: *Advocate, Out, Genre.* But in rural America, you take what you can get. Thank god for those fundamentalist groups always on the lookout for the homosexual hydra of gay pornography. If not for Edwin Meese's high-profile anti-obscenity commission, one of the lovely programs of the Reagan years, I wouldn't have known that queer porn existed. Thanks to him, I even knew what titles to look for.

And now I get to produce my own obscenities. In the past, I wondered if I was being a little too open, if I might be giving the Pat Robertson worshipers of the world more ammunition. But I certainly would rather have a young proto-queer in my hometown reading the benefits of being a bottom than choking down another selective interpretation of Leviticus.

I just wish I could have bought that copy of *Blueboy.* It would be far more relevant to my life than my high school yearbooks.

Don't You Want Me?

There are those who wonder (among them my mother and other family members still brave enough to stay in contact) if I purposefully insert myself into the embarrassing situations I so often write about.

Of course I do, but not for my own benefit. It's all for research, so I can provide you, the reader, with tips and rules that will make your life more rewarding and embarrassment-free.

Yeah, right.

But, given my propensity for unwittingly making a fool of myself, I suppose I should make the best of it by trying to help others avoid the same pitfalls. For example …

Not long ago, I took a few vacation days, and one evening I found myself in a bar with friends (the only real difference between a work night and a vacation night is that I don't have to call in sick the next morning). Joining us toward the end of the evening was a cute young thing that I've harbored a small crush on for the past few weeks.

In other words, I was burning with lust. After fueling my charm engine with another round from the bar, I began all the necessary preparations for the conquest.

I'm sure you've been there for the rest of the story: after you flirt industriously, thinking it's being returned, and spend a lot of money on refueling, he up and walks out the door with your best friend instead.

The worst part about this situation is that you are left with your other friends, who know precisely what just happened. And being gay friends, they are not going to let you forget. Ever.

These situations are exacerbated at after-hours parties. At 4:00 AM, everyone knows it's too late to go back to the bar to find another potential mate. Therefore, the competition for the ones on hand is fierce. But even if you always find yourself getting the short end of the stick at the end of the night, don't despair. There are some handy little tricks to help you win the battle for temporary affection.

Whenever your competition goes to the bathroom, casually take his seat next to your quarry. Strike up a quick conversation. However, don't be obvious. It's acceptable to talk about your home decor, but not to proudly mention the size of your bed.

One problem with this technique is that it can so easily be turned against you, particularly if you have a small bladder. If there are a number of competitions going on, as is usually the case at an after-hours party, the evening will degenerate into a roomful of drunken, lecherous queens playing an impromptu game of musical chairs.

If you find that you're unable to distract your prey from your friend, drastic steps must be taken. If you're in an apartment building, set off the fire alarm; in a private home, just set a fire. During the complete pandemonium that follows, show your powerful masculinity by rescuing your target from danger and whisking him away to the relative safety of your own home.

Hey, desperate times call for desperate measures.

Bad Trips

Among the many reasons I have chosen to live in the city, aside from my proximity to boy bars, is the lack of need for a car. In my opinion, if you can't walk it or take a five-dollar cab ride, why bother?

Still, I've found myself at times in a horrible situation that sometimes befalls the transportationally-challenged city dweller: tricking outside the city. Spending the night in a far-flung suburban housing development will make you wish for a car faster than grocery shopping in an urban Soviet Safeway.

Lest anyone think I'm trying to disrespect suburbanites, be assured that some of my best friends live in the outlying areas. However, a number of disastrous experiences with visits to the suburbs have left me somewhat biased (just call me an urbanist).

My problems with the city limits began during my first visit to DC, when a friend deserted me at a bar in order to get some quality-time with a cute blond thing he had just met (how could I blame him?). As a college boy three hours away from his dormitory room and desperate for a place to crash for the evening, I decided to use my new-meat wiles to grab the nearest potential host. I ended up with a used-car salesman at his parents' house in Leesburg. As a country boy who at the time still believed that cities were just compact towns, I naively thought that "just across the river" meant, well, "just across the river." In suburbanese, it really means "forty-five minutes if the traffic's good."

For mood music, my new and temporary friend put on the banjo theme from *Deliverance*. Oh, of course he didn't. But I am fairly sure I saw Bambi's mom mounted on the wall among all the other stuffed woodland creatures.

If you simply must go home with a suburbanite, remember the First Law of Suburban Tricking: you are trapped. If you decide you don't like what you've gotten, the lack of escape routes will force you to live with it for the next few hours. For example, the subway to Washington doesn't run in the wee hours; in other cities, it may be safer to stay put than risk boarding a train at 4:00 AM. To make things worse, suburban neighborhoods are not known for having three million unlicensed, dilapidated taxis roaming their streets looking for suckers to overcharge.

My first line of defense before agreeing to such a tryst is to negotiate a ride back to the city. The potential trick must agree to drive me straight to my doorstep at a reasonable hour in the morning or when I've had enough, whichever comes first. This way, I avoid the embarrassment of walking down the main strip on Sunday afternoon wearing the remains of my outfit from the previous night's underwear party. I can only imagine the nightmare of riding the train at 10:30 on Sunday morning with the well-dressed families on their way to church with their white, gilt-edged Bibles held tightly to their prim laps while they tell the children, "Don't even look at him."

Next, I determine the actual destination. Some men have tried to mislead me with the vaguest of references to the actual location where the tryst will take place, but I always demand specifics. Anything outside the Beltway is a definite no-no; residents of other cities will have to determine their own boundaries for how far they are willing to travel for a good time. I know of one queer boy who traveled forty miles into deepest, darkest, redneckiest Virginia for a fling, never to be heard from again—I expect to find "Have You Seen Me?" notices on cocktail glasses any day now.

When arriving at the appointed pseudo-townhouse apartment complex, I generally get the urge to run from the house as fast as I can, particularly when I see the picture of his wife and children, who are currently visiting family in the Midwest. When he asks if I need a daddy, the urge to bolt becomes overwhelming. If you find yourself in this situation, follow my lead: Grab the nearest cordless phone, lock yourself in the bathroom, and begin calling every automobile owner you know to beg for rescue. Of course, if your host owns only a tabletop, rotary-dial phone left over from the days of Ma Bell, you're screwed. Consider it a lesson.

An important note: all of this applies double when you bring home a suburban trick who lacks transportation. Shelling out fifty bucks for a taxi to the outlying Marine base will ruin your plans for Sunday brunch.

And for everyone who lives in the suburbs and beyond: I know you believe that those of us who live in cities with drive-by shootings, open-air drug markets, and aggressive panhandlers are far crazier than any suburbanites.

You're right.

Feel the Burn

"Is this the year?" my television keeps asking me, while showing Adonis-like bodies jogging down a beach and improving their muscles on the high-tech equipment available at Holiday Spa. My usual answer to this question is, of course, "Not in this lifetime."

Why should I shell out perfectly good money for the gym when I've developed my own workout program—one that allows me to both stay in shape and keep my social life active. I've put together some of the highlights for your own physical enhancement.

As always, you should consult your physician before starting any exercise regimen. Just don't tell him how many cocktails you have during the course of the week—you might find yourself involuntarily checked into a rehab program.

The Stomach Suck.

Whenever a nominally cute man comes within five to ten feet of you, attempt to reduce your waistline from thirty-four to twenty-nine by clenching your gut. If you go out often enough to locations known for the quality of their clientele, your abdominal muscles will perk up before you know it.

A warning: don't overexert yourself or you may find that your liver and kidneys have relocated to your throat.

Curl and Gulp.

This should be self-explanatory. You can get in more reps if you only frequent bars with really cheap drink specials.

Booger Check.

Very similar to the Curl and Gulp, but cheaper because it doesn't require a cocktail. Also similar to the Stomach Suck, because it's performed when in proximity to a cute boy. Maximize the benefits of the routine by twisting your upper body away as you perform the check, ostensibly so that no one will know what you're doing.

Don't perform too many reps or everyone will think you're wiping away major residue.

Pulse Palpitater.

An involuntary exercise your body performs whenever you spot a cute butt that looks even better than the one you visited with last night on the cover of *Rump* magazine.

Bathroom Dash.

Perfect for those with small bladders. For a more thorough workout, only visit bars where you have to take the stairs to the ladies' room. Again, be careful. If you run to the bathroom too often, people will start asking if they can come along.

The Psycho-Ex Sprint.

You will get a better workout if you don't run for the door when your mentally-unstable ex-boyfriend makes a sudden appearance. Instead, stay in the bar and try to avoid him for an hour or so. This works best in large clubs—in a small bar, you'll think you're running a marathon.

The Ten-Minutes-Before-Work Panic.

This is the most exercise you can get in so short a time. While still sleeping, turn off your alarm. When you realize what you've done, leap out of bed with all your remaining strength and tear through your morning routine at top speed (you may want to postpone the Massengill until the evening).

As you can see, this workout covers just about everything. Even the amenities of a gym hold no attraction for me. If I wanted steam-room action, I'd go to the bathhouse.

Cable Ready

What little capacity for productivity I have managed to retain through the past few years is now gone. You see, I finally got around to having the cable television reconnected. After about a year of mostly-sanitized network dialogue, I can finally hear the melodious sound of "fuck" emanating from my TV set.

I believe that I could get by with just four or five channels if they threw in the occasional profanity and nudity that serve as an indicator of really classy works of art. I still wonder why, when I have 145 cable channels, at any time of day I can find the same four-hour psychic network infomercial on half of them. [Just as an aside, the automatic spell checker on my computer just blithely skipped by the word "infomercial" as if nothing had ever happened, which perhaps says more about the state of American culture than my own cynical outlook ever could.]

When I was growing up, we had three channels (four if the weather was right, and five if you counted PBS).

This may seem limiting to children of the cable era, but at any time, each of those channels was showing a different program. I mean a really different program, not just a different repeat of the same show.

Of course, I had to turn the antenna to the appropriate point on the compass (and it had to be exceptionally fine-tuned to pick up *Star Trek*). And, predictably for western Kentucky, there was no plethora of gay programming. If anyone had suggested that we would have gay and lesbian sitcoms, the townspeople would have laughed uproariously at the notion while looking for the nearest tar and feathers.

Those who lived in Princeton, with its population of more than eight thousand and slightly more liberal views, got cable television fairly early on. In Fredonia, I heard that one of the town fathers (I think there were two, total) supposedly nixed the idea because, "We don't need those dirty movies comin' in here."

Speak for yourself, bucko, I thought.

The arrival of cable in Fredonia was a moot point for me, regardless, as I lived outside the city limits where it wasn't economical to run the wire. I had to use my imagination and limited resources to produce my own dirty movies in my mind.

Didn't you ever notice that Donny Osmond was really hot?

The children of the nineties are more fortunate than those of my generation—even those few who don't have cable have the *Mighty Morphin' Power Rangers*. The red, black, blue, and white Power Rangers are far better-looking than any of the live-action kiddie-show stars of my youth. *

Not to mention that their costumes are much more form-fitting.

During the Saturday mornings of my childhood, there were not that many cute boys gracing the big floor-model Zenith in the corner of the living room. The cute ones were all animated. However, the unreal nature of pen-and-ink drawings did nothing to detract from my attraction to Robin, who bravely battled the bad guys while clad in the skimpiest of Speedos. When one of the three television stations in my rural area began broadcasting the live-action *Batman* series, I found that Robin actually wore nylons. This only served to confirm that Robin was my kind of guy.

You can imagine my disappointment when I caught an episode of the more recent animated *Batman* series and found Robin clad in an outfit that covers him from head to toe. How can the Dynamic Duo ever hope to save the world when the Joker isn't distracted by the sight of Robin's beautiful, hairless legs?

But I digress …

With the lack of cute boys, the Saturday morning television shows of my youth had little to hold my attention (one exception being *Land of the Lost,* but that

---

* The children of the twenty-first century don't have to waste their time waiting for syndicated, teen-friendly hotness to arrive on the TV—they're all off downloading *hentai* from the Internet.

had dinosaurs and Sleestacks so it was easy to ignore the aesthetic lackings of the male stars). Bereft of proto-queer role models, I turned to the nearest available substitutes: Electra Woman and Dynagirl.

Armed with laser-firing bracelets, this female dynamic duo fought the forces of evil from their secret underground lair, traveling to the scene of the crime in their neat little three-wheeled car that converted into a mini-airplane. My best friend Sammy Jack and I were so entranced by the show that it was our primary role-playing game during recess (until I was old enough to watch *Charlie's Angels,* which is another story entirely). Unfortunately, I was always the one to play the role of Dynagirl, whose primary function was to be captured by the evildoer and saved by Electra Woman.

I have a sneaky suspicion that this has something to do with my being a bottom.

Video Ventures

As we all know, there are certain tricks of the trade when it comes to judging the compatibility of a potential mate, or in some cases, the wisdom of spending the night with someone whose name is Brian … or Ryan, or something like that. Many of these procedures are simple: looking for ice picks under the bed, searching for discreetly placed Maria Callas posters, checking the refrigerator for body parts.

Other methods require more contemplation, as different personality types can be interpolated from the most minute of clues. Videotape collections are an excellent example, particularly when it comes to the so-called "all-male" films. Therefore, watch for the following when perusing the porno collection of your intended.

The Collector.

This is not the sort of man who copies two porno movies from a friend and watches them repeatedly for two years. He prefers to have the real thing, oversized box and all. A good indication you have stumbled into the lair of this creature is the vastness of his collection—i.e., he owns the entire back catalog of Falcon, Catalina, and Colt studios, and his mailbox overflows with the latest XXX-rated flyers (*"Uncut Cops with Naughty Nightsticks,* only $19.95!!!"*).

Put any thoughts of an extended relationship out of your mind. After two rolls in the hay with him, you'll realize you'll never be able to perform the amazing feats of nimble nookie that play on a repeating loop in his fantasy-laden mind. Don't feel bad—most Olympic gymnasts wouldn't pass muster either.

The Off-Brand Man.

All the videos are produced by companies you never heard of, such as Puppy Productions (whose direct mail list, I suspect, bears suspicious similarity to the membership list of Transformation Ministries). If you see titles such as *Hand-le with Care,* be ready to make a trip to Safeway for Crisco Sticks. If you see something that features electro-anal stimulation, be sure to inquire about the wiring capacity of your new friend's apartment. It would be embarrassing to blow a fuse on the first date.

Out of Sight, Out of His Mind.

If you find his porno collection hidden behind such cinematic classics as *Fantasia* and *The Wiz,* begin looking for the nearest exit. He probably still has the underwear section of the Sears catalog hidden between his mattress and box spring.

Porno? What Porno?

Yeah, right. Most likely, he secreted the entire collection away in a double-locked chest in the basement. If it happens to be true and his abode is bereft of porno, don't even bother. Remember the rule: have none, get none.

And This One's Just Right.

This one has just enough to stay interested but no so much as to become obsessed. This is the type of man with whom you can have a relaxing evening at home watching movies and getting ideas.

And should you be wondering to which category I belong … it's not this one.

Not-so-Private Functions

E ven though the sun had yet to set, I was not all that surprised to see a man zipping up on Seventeenth Street as he walked away from a fresh splash mark on the side of a liquor store. After all, one gets used to these things. What surprised me was his sudden, boisterous scream, "Does it take you that fucking long to throw up?!"

Given the force behind his question, I assumed someone was taking care of business. Sure enough, across the street, a man was unloading his previously consumed Night Train into the corner bushes.

It's the little things that make life in DC such a hoot.

I must admit that I've been no angel when it comes to public displays of gastric explosions, though in my post-fraternity days I've managed to keep them confined to a few well-placed belches. In high school, I always kept such public displays within the confines of cow-pasture keg parties. (And in case you were wondering, we never went cow-tipping—that would have meant knocking all the rednecks off the cows' rumps.)

The last out-and-out public ralph that I remember involved eight shots of tequila, two gin and tonics, a black Russian, a bottle of Seagram's, a second-story window, and a group of unfortunate women's college students on the patio below. One thing I can say about stomach acid: it's a quick indicator of whether a hair color is real or imaginary.

Since that time, I've managed to keep my cookie-tossing under control when in public (it helps that I haven't again been tantalized with such tempting targets). Which makes it easy for me to proudly note that I have yet to throw up within the confines of a nightclub.

This has been a particular nightmare of mine—even I would have problems living down a reputation as "that queen who puked on the dance floor." This is not an idle worry, either. A few years ago at Tracks, I watched on the patio as a big-haired NoVa chick redefined projectile vomiting. I wouldn't be surprised if the management had to replace the wood. Actually, I would have felt sorry for her if I hadn't been so busy trying not to throw up from my own hysterical laughter.

Lest you wonder why on earth I would bring up such a gut-wrenchingly disgusting topic, let me assure you that there is a moral to this story: moderation is not only wise, it's usually far prettier.

A friend of mine did not seem to realize the importance of this life lesson when we attended an open-bar party at a local nightclub. Instead of enjoying the lovely spread of cocktail weenies and dips, he attempted to empty every beer fridge in the joint. The final blow came when he challenged me to a chug contest. I'm just thankful that the nice gentleman standing next to use didn't notice the new ornamentations on his cowboy boots, provided at the courtesy of my woozy friend.

Which leads to moral number two: periodically check your shoes—you never know where they've been.

The List

I'm sure everyone has heard, and most likely used, the phrase, "You're on my list." For those unsure how to begin a list of their own, I've decided to share my list—however, given space constraints, I will only be able to reveal a small portion.

—First, anyone who has ever held an elevator door to allow another person time to get on the elevator, when said other person is still about a hundred yards from the door. These people are listed twice when, at the time of the infraction, three other elevators are waiting, empty, in the lobby.

—All those guys who chatted with me in a bar, only to suddenly pull the "Oh, I've got to run to the bathroom," and either not invited me along or never returned.

—My substitute teacher from seventh grade who mispronounced my name on the roll as, "Sin." She may have been accurate, but that's beside the point.

—Cab drivers who attempt to engage me in conversation.

—Anyone who has ever asked me, "Have you gained a little weight?"

—People who double-park just one car length away from a double-sized open spot. Also in this category are those people who sit outside on Sunday morning honking their horn for their worship buddy to come out. I would assume that, as church-going folk, these people would realize God gave them legs so they could get out of the damn car and ring the doorbell.

—Anyone who has ever, upon hearing that I was from Kentucky, immediately looked down to see if I was wearing shoes.

—My first three bosses—although due to potential legal ramifications I can't elaborate on this any further than pointing out that my tenure under them was a pure, unadulterated, living hell.

—Family members who have asked me, "So, have you met any nice girls up in DC?"

—That guy who said, "But with lube and poppers, you won't even know it's in there."

—My former boyfriend who once borrowed my wallet and said, "Trust me."

—The bartender in Oklahoma City who wouldn't accept my ID because it didn't have a "state seal." Warning to any airport bartenders out there: do not attempt to stop me from having a beer when I've been traveling all day. I know many creative and damaging uses for an empty popcorn basket.

—Those people who have decided I can't smoke anywhere in an airport in the few minutes I have remaining before I enter a multi-ton vehicle that has the potential to become a flaming comet of death.

—People on the street who ask me if I know Jesus.

—People who come to my front door to ask me if I know Jesus.

—Relatives who ask me if I know I'm on the fast track to Hell.

—The girl from eighth grade who turned all my friends against me and left me to eat lunch by myself for one whole year.

—People who live in the past and bring up ancient slights and transgressions that are best left forgotten.

Uh oh.

Spring Rules

Spring has sprung once again, bringing with it the inevitable allergies. I speak not, of course, of pollen, but of the fashion and behavior disasters that occur each year when all the queers get ecstatic about the end of winter but can't take possession of their beach houses until after Memorial Day.

Allergy remedies line the aisles of pharmacies, promising protection from the unpleasant mating habits of trees, grass, and flowers. Unfortunately, the only thing that can cure the allergic reaction I have to certain queer springtime actions (whether related to physical urges or not) is that those committing the infractions cease and desist immediately.

In order to make life more pleasant for everyone, I've put together a few rules of conduct for spring. My personal happiness, of course, is merely a fortunate by-product.

Rule #1: If you buy a pair of Rollerblades and consistently fall on your ass, make sure to practice somewhere within my vicinity. I could use the laugh.

Rule #2: Just because you have a membership at the gym doesn't mean you should dress like the men featured in the ads. You have to do more than pay monthly dues if you want to wear a Lycra tank top.

Rule #3: Don't wear Lycra tank tops.

Rule #4: White tennis shoes should be worn at the gym, on the tennis court, or with reasonable-length shorts. They should not be worn with jeans.*

A corollary: white tennis shoes should actually be white, not just white shoe laces with three thousand square inches of the manufacturer's logo.

Rule #5: If your skin begins to look like a special effect worthy of an Academy Award, you should lay off the tanning bed for a couple of weeks.

Rule #6: If one or both of your butt cheeks bulge from the back of last year's hot pants, change.

Rule #7: If you wear sandals, do not cover your feet with anything other than sandals. What the hell is the point of either crunchy-chewy or designer sandals if you're going to wear super-thick scrunchy socks with them? Let your toes breathe for god's sake. If you show up wearing black socks with sandals, you will be docked five points. If you show up wearing sandals and white athletic socks with colored stripes around your calves, you will be docked twenty points.

---

*   The fact that I began violating this rule sometime after I turned thirty should not in any way reflect on the validity of these rules as a whole. Rules were made to be broken. Except the one about Lycra tank tops.

Rule #8: Don't assume that everyone wants to know about your fabulous beach house. And if you go on an equally fabulous, globe-spanning vacation, don't tell me about it unless you bought me something.

Rule #9: Remember to spread your sick days over different days of the week. Bosses tend to figure out your Thursday night habits when you miss five Fridays in a row.

Rule #10: Whether you're a courier or just a queer boy out for a stroll, you must wear a jockstrap with bike shorts. Exceptions can be made for exceptionally cute and hung men—all exceptions must be approved by me, in person. Be prepared to present your qualifications in both categories.

Rule #11: If you must wear cologne or other scents, ease off a bit until the temperature goes down. It's bad enough that everyone in town is slinging sweat drops at every turn. It's worse when everyone is slinging designer-scented sweat drops. After thirty seconds on an elevator, all the passengers come out smelling like a Macy's perfume counter after a bomb exploded.

Rule #12: This should be common knowledge by now, since it's been put forth every year by myself and many others, but surprisingly it's not. Never, under any circumstances, tell me that the reason it's so humid in DC is that the city is built on a swamp. I've heard this. I need to hear it again about as much as I need to be told that the earth revolves around the sun or that Michael Jackson and Bubbles are "just friends."

As a corollary to this rule, please don't tell me that it's hot enough to "fry an egg on the sidewalk." If so, who cares? Go try and cook your breakfast out front and tell me about it when you're finished.

Rule #13: I beg of the women out there reading—don't wear pantyhose when it's 90-plus degrees outside with a heat index of 110. I get a heat rash just looking at your legs.

And yes, this goes for drag queens too. If you ever expect to be fabulous, you're going to have to learn to shave that close anyway.

Kiss, Kiss

Recently, I went to one of those gay events where our self-appointed pillars of the community run around pretending to like each other. One of those pillars that I had recently interviewed approached me with a huge smile, saying, "I'm so glad to see you." Before I could concoct an appropriate response, I found myself in a bigger hug than my mother ever gives me. So, assuming he must have really liked the article, I did what seemed natural in such a situation.

I gave him a quick peck on the cheek.

I only did this because I thought I had one coming myself. When my mouth greeting was not returned, I felt embarrassed. *What if he thinks I'm flirting? Maybe he's disgusted. Oh my god, he'll never return my phone calls now!*

As you can probably guess, I've never quite gotten the hang of social kissing.

You've probably been in this situation yourself. Run into a crowd of friends at the local bar and you can get face cramps from the amount of puckering you must perform in your greeting ritual. Should you run into them after four or five cheap cocktails, you'll find yourself covered in enough saliva to digest a four-course meal.

In my attempt to discern which kisses are appropriate for which situations, I've assembled the following list.

Straight to the Cheek.

Use this for someone you don't know well. This is particularly good to use with a former trick whose name you can't quite remember. I've also found it the most appropriate kiss when forced to kiss someone you hate. Generally, when someone kisses my cheek, I assume that I fall into one of these categories, though it's possible they just don't appreciate the fine scent of a Marlboro.

A Peck on the Lips.

This is the standard greeting for someone you consider to be a friend, or a person you slept with and still talk to (including ex-boyfriends).

The problem with this kiss is that too many people assume that I consider them a friend—I find myself going for his cheek while he goes for my mouth. It makes both of us look like those little dunking birds my grandmother kept on her windowsill. After this awkward ritual, I usually end up kissing his ear, which reinforces his mistaken idea that I like him.

Going for the Jugular.

Perhaps he has an Anne Rice fixation. Or maybe he fancies the taste of expensive cologne (because of course you would only wear the best). Frankly, it just gives me the creeps.

A Slip of the Tongue.

If, as he gives me a quick peck on the lips to say good-bye, he briefly slips his tongue into my mouth, I assume he's "interested." Of course, he may just be interested in what I had for dinner.

Full-on, Open Mouth.

This generally occurs later in the evening (or the afternoon if you happen to be taking advantage of daytime drink specials). If you allow it to go on for more than two seconds, it is time to make a decision: take him home or take him to the women's room.

Disco Fredonia

When I was a young lad, disco took over my home town of Fredonia, Kentucky.

This was back when people thought *Saturday Night Fever* was a good movie. I certainly thought it was. It was John Travolta who inspired me to wear a tan polyester J.C. Penney's suit and brown satin shirt to my first school dance.

I've been a fashion queen from way back when.

Anyway, disco didn't conquer Fredonia by sending in troops of raving Village People fans. Instead, disco came through a much more traditional means: my parents.

In an itsy-bitsy farm town, people are often searching for something to do. [Insert your own farm animal joke here.] Perhaps inspired by the constant flow of Donna Summer from the radio, my parents banded together with other like-minded couples and signed up for disco dancing lessons.

For a little boy who loved to dance around his bedroom to the sounds of Abba and Andy Gibb, the first two albums I ever purchased with my own money, this was an event of stellar proportions. I knew that if my parents learned to do the Manhattan Boogie, I couldn't be far behind.

Once a week, my parents and their friends would pile into their cars for the forty-five minute drive to the disco studio in Paducah—sort of a seventies wagon train. Then, on the weekend, they would take turns hosting disco practice parties in their respective semi-finished basements.

Of course, I wasn't allowed to go to Paducah with them (I never understood why ten-year-olds can't get into clubs if all they want to do is dance; if the club had just served Mountain Dew, I would have been fine). I was, however, allowed to hang out at the practice parties in various basement rec rooms. As our one-story house had a two-foot crawl space in lieu of a basement, a practice session always gave me the chance to go out for the evening.

Although no one ever bothered to hang a glittering disco ball from the various low ceilings, in my head, those basements were full-fledged nightclubs. Some substitutions were necessary, such as the turntable with an automatic changer ("Play up to seven albums at once!") that filled in as a DJ. But there was beer for the men and piña coladas for the ladies, so I believed it was close enough.

The only compromise I didn't like was having my little sister for a dance partner. Being a straight country girl, she was not born with the innate ability to follow the beat of Gloria Gaynor as I was. That's why I preferred the line dances.

In fact, the only good disco partner I found was my sixth-grade girlfriend, Glenda. We tore up the floor during our class talent show, wowing them with our disco moves. After that, we led the entire unwitting classroom in a production number of "YMCA." (This was before someone's parents finally figured out what the words meant.) I still have a congratulatory note from my teacher addressed to "Sean 'Disco Daddy' Bugg."

I probably would have discoed even better if I hadn't spent the whole performance wondering what it would be like if my friend Steve were my partner.

Too bad I had to wait so long to find out the answer to that question.

Shy Guy

People always act surprised when I tell them I consider myself a shy person. "Your columns are more revealing than wet underwear in a porno movie," they say. "That's not shy."

While these people display a good grasp of the symbolism contained in Falcon movies, they unfortunately do not understand shyness as a condition. You can be shy and still be a writer. I can even handle doing radio. But put me where I know a crowd of people can see my face, and I develop a sudden case of lockjaw (one reason to keep the lights off if I'm at an orgy).

I suspect that the people who refuse to believe my shyness are the same people who, as teenagers, had no problem making speeches to the class or asking someone to dance. Of course, they never had to ask anyone to dance since they always had a date.

In other words, it's a shy thing, you wouldn't understand.

Over the years I have learned to control my shy impulses, particularly after I got my tetracycline prescription in high school (the Oxy 10 just wasn't doing it). The sight of a fresh, clean, and only slightly-blemished face gave me the courage to put on my best Chess King outfit, splash on some Jovan musk and head out to the nearest high school dance. Alone.

I had a wonderful time, even for a little in-the-closet proto-queer. If I saw a girl without a redneck boyfriend, I asked her to dance. To my joyful surprise, the girls said yes.

I found myself working my way up the high school social ladder, asking progressively more popular girls to dance. I had passed by the marching band flag corps and the student council members. There was only one social level left: cheerleader.

I walked right up, confident in my newfound aura of maleness, and asked a cheerleader (the long-haired blond one) to join me.

"No," she said, turning her back on me.

My short-lived macho ego effectively crushed, I returned to being a shy guy for, oh, ten years or so.

I had hoped that when I joined the gay community, my shyness would fall away like the pupa from the butterfly, allowing my true inner beauty to run free among the caring, loving, and warm-hearted people of my community.

After a couple of years living in Washington I finally got a reality check: the only time you can be guaranteed unconditional love from a complete stranger is on Pride Day or at 3:00 AM when you're both desperate.

I'm not bitter about the reality of the situation. Being queer does not automatically make one brilliant, beautiful, and saintly (though it may improve the odds a bit). Which means that shy guys like myself will continue to stand to the side in the bars, watching from the corners of our eyes, hoping that the cute boy across the crowd is bold enough to make the first move.

So, should you run across me hiding in the corner, be kind. Be gentle. Be understanding. But most of all, if you want to loosen me up, buy me a cocktail.

A vodka tonic works much better than Oxy 10.

Frat Boys

During my first year in a fraternity, anyone from the real world would have caught the hint that something was just a little repressed about those boys.

Each year, the entire pledge class was divided into groups of four and sent on scavenger hunts in distant locations. My group was sent to my future home, Washington DC, along with instructions to find various items, including a dildo and KY jelly.

See what I mean?

Enterprising young thing that I was, as well as desperate to ingratiate myself to the fraternity members who had provided me with an instant social life during my first week at school, I led our pack to the Pleasure Chest in Georgetown. It was easy enough to find the dildo, but they unfortunately did not stock KY. In a moment of divine inspiration, I substituted another lubricant labeled "Anal Glow."

Had my pledge brothers not been so busy making gleeful fun of all the "homosexual" items in the store, they might have caught on to an important fact about me.

Regardless, the dildo went on to occupy a hallowed place within my fraternity. We discovered that, if applied to the Sunday funnies, it would pick up a lovely image of Lucy on its head, just like Silly Putty. With a little spit on the base, it made a wonderful hanging ornament for the window in the dormitory hall. My closest pledge brothers spent an evening taking pictures of themselves and the dildo in homoerotic poses, i.e. hanging out of one guy's button-fly jeans and angling toward another's open mouth.

This was all, of course, in fun.

Then again, homosexuality was a consistently entertaining topic for my brothers. What do you expect from a small Southern university that was all-male for more than two hundred years and was named, in part, after Gen. Robert E. Lee?

One of the most affectionate nicknames they developed for a brother was "Sac," as in scrotum. They talked about their buttholes more than the attendees of a bottoms' convention.

They loved watching fags on MTV. Whenever little Jimmy Somerville appeared, they would all yell "It's the Pocket Fag!" For Morrissey, they yelled "It's the Mopey Fag!"

As one of the only open liberals in a rabidly conservative student body, it fell to me to play defense for the suspected homosexuals at school. My willingness to stand up (somewhat) for the objects of my frat brothers' derision earned me my own nickname: the Aficionado.

Predictably, my secret eventually got out, and I was "asked" to leave, since homosexuality was incompatible with fraternity life, even though no one had a picture of me with a dildo in my mouth. Actually, I think they were upset because they knew I had slept with a some of the brothers, and I wouldn't give them the names.

I left behind the first dildo, our pledge class mascot. It had disappeared after someone stuck it on a car belonging to a member of a rival fraternity. I received sporadic reports of dildo appearances. One person swore he saw a dog carrying the dildo across campus. He assumed it must have been buried, perhaps next to Gen. Lee's horse, Traveller.

If so, I'm glad the dildo found its place in history.

Gang Bang

Recently, a good friend of mine has found himself stumbling into parties where, after the initial cocktail, clothes start to come off—outside the bedroom, if you know what I mean. Considering the fact that he has not invited me to join these impromptu nude parties, I'm not so sure about his status as a *good* friend anymore.

Actually, I'm never surprised to hear about three-ways and four-ways popping up across the city. In fact, they seem to be as common as unfortunate fashion accidents at a nightclub. However, I've been hearing more about parties of five or more as of late. Therefore, I've put together some tips and hints to make your gathering come off just right.

The Guest List.

Careful thought should go into the development of a guest list for your party. This is not the type of event for which you want all your friends handing out invitations at a bar. Give all of your invitations verbally—if accepted, write your address on a cocktail napkin or some other handy surface (the more you use your imagination with this, the more likely it is that he will show up).

Remember, you don't want your party to be like a trip to the bathhouse where you constantly have to swat away eager hands that suddenly materialize from the dark, so don't be afraid to be picky in your choices. If you wouldn't have sex with him in private, you certainly don't want to do it in front of ten of your closest friends.

Make sure to get some diversity in the crowd, finding some men that could appeal to a wide range of guests. After all, everyone likes a broad selection.

Of course, the guest list should include someone skilled in orgy etiquette—I myself am available on a freelance basis.

Things to Provide.

You may want to visit the local Price Club to buy bulk condoms. If your plans for the party include a sexual smorgasbord in which everyone takes a little sample of your rump roast, these are a requirement.

Following this train of thought, you wouldn't serve fried chicken without napkins, so don't forget to provide your guests with plenty of towels. In fact, given the possibility of unfortunate accidents, you may want to provide lemon-scented Handi-Wipes and mark a path to the nearest shower.

It will also be helpful if you place a number of small wastebaskets around the room(s) in convenient locations for the disposal of the accouterments of the party. Without these, your visiting mother may find quite a surprise when she checks under your couch for dust bunnies.

Stop Means Stop.

If you've handled your guest list correctly, none of your guests should find themselves in the uncomfortable situation of saying *no* to another guest. But they may find themselves trying to say *stop* to a particularly enthusiastic one. Should you find one of your guests in this situation, be a gracious host and step in. The following simple line said with a smile should do it: "I think he's running a bit low. Would you like to try a little piece of mine?"

Book Worm

I started reading at an early age, before starting first grade. During the afternoons, I could usually be found at Granny's, hunkered over the funny pages, willfully sounding out each and every word in *Beetle Bailey, Steve Canyon,* and *The Family Circus.*

From my memory, I skipped way beyond the average reading level for my age group. I was still in elementary school when I discovered my mom's paperback copy of Stephen King's *The Shining.* My parents thought it was cute that I was pretending to read "big people's books"— had they realized that I understood the book perfectly well, I'm sure they would have taken the book and saved me from my years-long fear of closed shower curtains.

Between *Star Wars* and Stephen King, my reading habits for the next few years were set in stone (on trips to the mall, my parents just dumped me at Readmore bookstore; no candy-cane-wielding pervert could lure me away from racks of books—I hadn't hit puberty yet, so it worked). I even began writing my own horror / sci-fi stories, with my first published work appearing in my eighth-grade student newspaper. Of course, it was one of those stories that I think every pimply-faced, slightly overweight, slightly sissy twelve-year-old boy writes: The world ends in a giant cataclysm in just under three hundred words.

I had a little bit to learn about characterization.

Noticing my literary ambitions, Granny bought me an old Royal manual typewriter, the wonderful kind where you have to slam the carriage back at the end of each line, all the *o*'s and *e*'s look exactly alike, and your fingers grow strong from hitting highly resistant keys. To this day, I find myself pounding the hell out of my keyboard, as if I'm punishing it for not coming up with something funnier.

I'm typing *really* hard right now.

I tried my hand at numerous sci-fi stories, which I dutifully submitted to small magazines. They were dutifully returned, though the editors, perhaps having pity on such a young, misguided child, usually sent along a nice encouraging note.

I'm sure it was a stretch to be encouraging toward a thirteen-year-old who was writing stories about a baby surviving in a snowbound car wreck by eating its mother and father.

Of course, as I got older my interests began to differ. I found my mother's copy of *The Boys in the Mailroom*, a wonderfully trashy novel by the author of *Beaches* that includes a scene in which a teenage boy realizes his homosexuality by getting a blow job in a hall closet.

That particular section was marked and the book somehow found its way underneath my bed, for easy access when I needed some special 3:00 AM reading material.

By the time I graduated from high school and realized I was still having a problem with characterization, I went the traditional journalism route, hoping to hone my skills by writing about the rich, the powerful, and the sleazy.

At least I got that last one down.

Shower Shot

Women are far better prepared to meet the world than their male counterparts. Don't get me wrong—I certainly don't want to imply that women do not face myriad obstacles to becoming fully-valued members of society: glass ceilings, lower salaries, and beer-bellied husbands permanently attached to La-Z-Boys being a few of the most common.

But when it comes to having certain important questions answered, women get all sorts of information. Particularly that information that pertains to feminine hygiene. More specifically, it used to be that tampon, maxi-pad, and douche commercials ran primarily during the daytime soaps and talk shows. No longer. Now feminine hygiene commercials approach car ads in frequency.

I bring this up to illustrate an important aspect of growing up as a gay man: no one wants to talk about male hygiene. As a budding teenager wondering exactly how everything would work when I finally escaped my "heterosexual" upbringing, a little hygiene education would have been nice.

Imagine how much easier things would have been if one day I had seen a commercial in which two men, sitting around after a strenuous game of racquetball, casually discussed the benefits of the new Shower Shot.

"You know, Steve, I just haven't been feeling as fresh and clean lately."

"Well, Bruce, I've found the best way to solve that problem." Steve reaches into his bag and whips out a long, flexible, stainless steel tube with a tapered spout attached to one end. "Just hook this lemon-scented baby up in the locker room, and you'll be ready for anything."

"Wow, thanks, Steve."

"And don't forget, it comes with a special Shower Massage attachment for those nights you want to feel fresh but don't feel like going out."

Don't you think this would be a much more fun commercial than two guys shopping for a Volkswagen? Face it: we're born knowing how to shop, but other things we have to pick up along the way.

I actually figured out that douching could also apply to men by watching porno movies. However, as with any knowledge obtained from pornography, it lacked in realism. I'm assuming that the "actors" were putting the water in well before the scene started (and I'm still not sold on the wisdom of putting a garden hose up one's butt). Obviously, it didn't take more than a cursory understanding of the human digestive process to realize that all the anal washing I was watching had been preceded by at least two preparatory cleanings.

Not that I want to see the real thing (though if I wanted to, I'm sure it's available in another section of the video store back room or on its own special web site). There is such a thing as too much reality.

Coming Home

Christmas (a.k.a. the holiday season) is fraught with precarious situations, including trying to find a boyfriend in time for the most prestigious cocktail party and then breaking up with him before you're forced to buy him a present.

As problematic as that situation may be, however, there is another situation that strikes fear into my heart each December.

Going home to Kentucky.

Of course, it's not as though I don't love my family—I do, and very much. It's just that I'm—well, I don't quite fit in anymore in those country places where I grew up.

I had a preview of things to come when I passed through my hometown on a work assignment. I was surprised that I would ever find myself returning home for work—more surprising was the fact that I was there to teach a workshop on HIV/AIDS prevention.

Big city folks, even those of us who grew up on farms, tend not to understand why these topics aren't everyday dinner table conversation in Fredonia. You have to remember: this is a town in which almost no one understood why I began laughing hysterically when I saw a "nightclub" named "Nuttin' Butt Fun."

I thought the Fist Fuckers of America had opened up a chapter in my hometown.

Most of my relatives have an idea what I do for a living and, in general, seem happy that I've found something to do with my life. * They just don't want to get into specifics. It's because of this desire to converse with me on a need-to-know basis that the Bugg family tells everyone that I "talk at people" for a living.

Who am I to argue with that?

When the day of my workshop finally arrived, Granny helped me out by making the one-and-a-half hour drive to the city with me. I suppose I could have avoided the impending near-disaster if I had bothered to get my driver's license renewed. (If you had a choice between spending your day off cavorting in Dupont Circle or dealing with surly motor vehicle employees, what would you do? That's what I thought.)

Under the impression that Granny would be spending her time in the city exploring one of the malls, I had

---

*   Although a number of them persist in the delusion that I'm a reporter for the *Washington Post*. I finally decided to let them labor under that assumption since it means they believe I'm a decent writer.

agreed to let her come along. But when we arrived, she declared she would rather just wait in the hotel conference center until I finished.

Always quick on my feet, I quickly encamped her in the hotel bar/restaurant, and made frequent, nervous visits to check on her as the time for my workshop drew near. All seemed fine when I finally stepped before the audience to make my opening remarks.

Just as my co-presenter began explaining rectal gonorrhea as a surrogate marker for HIV infection in a population, I saw my grandmother sitting in the back, paying close attention.

I'm not completely clear what happened after that, but I've been told I did not have the heart attack I expected. After realizing the discomfort her presence caused me, she left the room. I'm sure watching her stuttering grandson talk about the male sex industry was none too comfortable for her, either.

Afterward, someone told me he was impressed that I could continue to do my work, even with my grandmother present.

Myself, I'm more impressed that I'm able to lead my life in the same situation. On some level, I'm sure Granny agrees.

Marry Me?

One of my favorite things to tell my friends and family during my high school years was that I planned to never get married. Adopting a pseudo-hip, free-to-be-me attitude, I proclaimed that marriage wasn't a relevant thing in today's modern world and if two people wanted to spend their time together, they didn't need the knot of marriage to do it for them.

What I was actually doing was preparing everyone for the soon-to-come day when they would all realize the real reason why I was never going to marry. Or, at least, marry a girl.

Surprisingly, the hints didn't work all that well (except for Mom, who stereotypically knew about me even before I was sure). In the grand scheme of things, it hasn't been that long since my relatives stopped asking if I had met any nice girls up in Washington.

Given the importance of maintaining a teenage heterosexual façade, I'm proud to report that I didn't use too many women to provide cover for my burgeoning sexuality (I saved that particularly nasty trick for college—my sincere apologies to Nancy, Carol, and that blonde girl from the community college on the other side of the mountain). But if I hadn't used at least a handful of women to hide my queerness, I would have ended up doing something reckless like actually marrying one.

Besides, I really liked most of the women I hung out with back home, so I wouldn't have wanted to punish them with a marriage to a closeted homo, even if I could offer them really helpful fashion tips (I was an early crusader against big hair).

There were plenty of other tricks to make people think I was heterosexual, or at least think I wasn't that big of a sissy. This was a challenge, as I had spent so much time reading books in full view of my peers. I overcame that by loaning everyone the paperback books I got from my mom's bookcase, with all the naughty parts marked (excluding a Judith-Krantzy novel called *The Boys in the Mailroom*, in which I had marked the only hot man-man sex scene I had been able to find—that was just for me).

Another trick was to make friends with football players. That way, any attack against my masculinity was an attack against theirs—a television show based on my high school years could be titled *My So-Called Détente*. Interestingly, the only time this defense system actually called on physical violence was when some redneck punched me because—get this—he thought I was hitting on his girlfriend.

Face it, I was good.

The final piece of my defense can be boiled down to five words: Led Zeppelin and Mötley Crüe. Cruising around Fredonia and Princeton in my fire-engine red 1976 Firebird, challenging rednecks to drag races on Main Street, and blasting "Shout at the Devil" and "Kashmir" from my stereo system did wonders for my heterosexual quotient. Just to cement things, I would occasionally play "Lick it Up" by Kiss and wear bandanas on my wrist—it was the early eighties, after all.

Just for the record, I drew the line at pants identified by the words "leather" or "parachute." It has never been cool to look like Sammy Hagar.

A Bitch in Time

O kay, everybody. Listen up.

From this point forward, I will be taking no excuses. This queer time thing has got to stop, if for no other reason than to save my own sanity (as well as that of all my other perpetually-early brothers).

I suppose it has something to do with me being a Capricorn (or just incredibly anal-retentive), but I can't stand being late for any appointment that takes place after, say, 11:00 AM or involves a deadline. Hey, I may be anal, but I'm certainly not a morning person—I'm talking social time here.

When I agree to meet someone for drinks or another social event, I generally show up a few minutes early. Then, after I've sat at my little table for more than an hour, looking like a fool while drinking approximately a six pack of beer and reading the sequel to *Jurassic Park* (or, even worse on the geek alert scale, the latest issue of *PC Computing*), the person who has wasted my valuable time will saunter in and ask, "Haven't you ordered me a drink?"

Luckily, happy hour drinks are cheap, so I can afford to throw more than one.

Punctual gay men are forced to pretend to be on queer time for any major social event. If someone invites you to a cocktail party at 8:00 PM, what time do you go? Depending on how fashionable you desire to be, anywhere between 10:30 PM and midnight (the ultra-fashionable will arrive at 5:30 AM, saying "Well, we just knew you would have cocktails for a fabulous after-hours party!").

As a result, I have to force myself to stay in my own home until the true start of the party. I'm usually dressed and coiffed far before then, so I can't do anything to disturb all the work that I've put into my appearance. And you can't go to the bar to kill time, because everyone else is still at home figuring out what they're going to wear.

This leaves me with nothing to do other than sit very still on the couch, having a few preparatory beers and watching Susan Powter infomercials. And people wonder why I'm so damn sullen when they see me out.

I'm also tired of having to tell my friends to show up at 7:00 when I really want them there by 9:00. I hate having to be duplicitous just to keep my life on schedule.

So, for all those believers in queer time out there, take a deep breath, click your heels together three times, and repeat after me: "I will be on time, I will be on time, I will be on time."

That wasn't so hard, was it? And I expect you to follow through. I'll be there to check on you.

Unless something suddenly comes up. But I'm sure you'll understand.

Too Much Information

One of the best reasons to hang out in a bar and throw back a few cocktails, aside from the possibility of getting laid, is the opportunity to chat with friends. Conversations generally become more interesting in direct proportion to the number of cocktails consumed.

There does come a saturation point during the outing, at which the conversation is conducted in special languages only the speakers understand. But even unintelligible conversation can be quite riveting, particularly if you have a side bet going on which participant will fall off his barstool first.

The only problem I've found with cocktail conversation is that it often leads to revelations I could do without. For unknown reasons, drunken queens feel compelled to supply far more details than even the most perverse among us would want to know.

Even more frightening are those queens who make such revelations after drinking nothing more than club soda and a twist of lime. At least we drunkards have an excuse.

As Miss Manners would gladly point out, there are reasons society has developed such concepts as "privacy" and "secrecy." So, to help those out there who may be confused by how much detail they should reveal in their conversations, I've gathered some examples as to what constitutes too much information. And if I think it's too much, what would your mother think?

Enough: "Bob and I have a sexually experimental relationship. We love to try as many new things as possible."

Too much: "Bob and I are really into nostril fucking. By the way, do you have a tissue on you?"

Enough: "I really have to go to the bathroom."

Too much: "Excuse me, I have to go to the bathroom before my colon blows chunks all over the floor."

Enough: "Why don't we have a three-way with that guy in the corner?"

Too much: "Because I haven't been attracted to you for the past year."

Enough: "I have problems getting along with my family. They've never accepted me for who I am."

Too much: "My family lives in my basement freezer. Mother's always loved the cold."

Enough: "Thanks, I'd love a cocktail."
Too much: "Just don't expect me to buy you one, too."

Enough: "I consider myself to be somewhat of a clean freak."
Too much: "My Shower Shot has to work overtime."

Enough: "I prefer to worship in the privacy of my own home. Perhaps you'd like to join me sometime?"
Too much: "You won't even have to slit the cat's throat."

Enough: "Sorry, I just don't feel like doing that tonight."
Too much: "Remember that Mexican dinner we had? It's on its way out."

Enough: "Jim, can you run to the bathroom with me for a minute?"
Too much: "I'm not sharing a damn thing with the rest of you, so don't even ask."

Enough: "It's not you, it's me."
Too much: "*You* make *me* sick."

Twosomes

As we all know, stereotypes about gay folks are bad. That's primarily because the stereotypes held by heterosexuals are so ludicrous they serve no function in the real world. Which is why I enjoy the stereotypes we come up with ourselves: they're much more accurate and fun.

Where would we be without labels such as Gymbot, Sugardaddy, and Dick 'o Death? In pretty dire straits, I believe.

Unfortunately, we tend to limit our types to individuals—when there are many more types out there to be defined. To help things along, I've put together a few types of gay couples you're likely to see while prowling the bars.

The Snuggle-Bunnies.

You can't miss this couple when they decide to venture out and show the world just how in wuv they are. Holding hands, rubbing backs, nuzzling into the other's neck—no cute display of affection is too disgusting for these two.

Try to avoid having dinner with them, as you most likely will have to throw up or have an emergency injection of insulin.

Just be careful not to confuse this couple with that other archetype of true love …

The Sex Fiends.

These boys are somewhat similar to the Snuggle-Bunnies, except for the fact they don't care if people can tell how in love they are. They want you to know just how hot they are for each other, and they can grope to prove it. This couple can be hard to spot, because they often look like any two random guys getting ready to embark on a really fun trick or a trip to the large bathroom stall.

Since there is nothing subtle about them, you know exactly what's going on every time one of them puts his hands underneath the table. Be careful getting out of a booth shared with these two—there's no telling what you may get on your pants.

The Ab-Masters.

Basically, this is the gymbot times two. When they take their shirts off—and they will—you get the feeling that when they have sex they fantasize about crunches, squats, and that fabulous new piece of equipment at the gym. If they happen to also be Snuggle-Bunnies, then you're seeing the next (now defunct) Rod and Bob Jackson-Paris business partnership. If they happen to be Sex Fiends, they will probably show up in a Colt film coming soon to a video store near you.

Three's Company.

This is the hardest couple to spot, as they are rarely seen together in the bar, which is their natural habitat. Instead, each circulates separately through the bar looking for someone good enough to share. There should be a rule requiring both partners in this type of relationship be together at all times. That way, the young innocent who receives the proposition could make a fully informed choice. This also helps avoid the embarrassment of having the intended run away screaming when introduced to the other partner.

Tongue Lashers.

When single, which is often, these two would be known as Bitchy Bitter Queens. Even love can't change everything.

Oh, Shut Up

As everyone knows, intelligent and cogent conversation does not exist within the confines of nightclubs and after-hours parties. And it's even harder to carry on a conversation the next morning when you're thinking, "What the hell is his name, anyway? And where did that bottle of maple syrup come from?"

Still, even with my lowered expectations for discourse, the depths of the inane chatter I am subjected to constantly amazes me. Therefore, I feel it necessary to issue a moratorium on the following tidbits, clichés, and flat-out stupidities.

"I can't believe you don't have a boyfriend."

I hear this more often than "Amen" from the back pew of a Baptist church. I believe the people who use this god-awful line are the same ones who run around the city telling everyone, "Well, you know why he doesn't have a boyfriend, don't you? You mean you haven't heard? Let me tell you about [*any random, ludicrous event from my recent past*]."

Being a resident of Washington DC, the nation's breeding ground for spin doctors, I've come up with my own damage-control line: "You may have heard some really strange things about me, but I'm on Prozac now and everything's fine." If it doesn't get me a boyfriend, at least I might find someone to split a prescription with.

"*He's just a friend.*"

If anyone tells you this, rest assured that the friend has harbored an obsessive love for the past three years. You have only two choices: run away or submit to a tension-filled three-way.

"*This is the VIP area. Do you have an invitation?*"

The next time you hear this one, take a long, hard look around. Do you see anyone who actually qualifies as a VIP? (No fair looking in the mirror.) In DC, for example, everyone believes themselves important, regardless how pointless their existence may be. Of course, when you do get in, you're forced to listen to everyone whine about how much better New York is or, worse, their plans to move to Miami.

"*I'd really like to take you home and fuck you.*"

This direct line might work if you're a Versace model visiting from South Beach, but otherwise, don't bring it near me. Guys who say this usually don't even bother to spring for a cocktail first. Save the porno-fantasy dialogue for the bathhouse.

"*Why haven't I slept with you yet?*"

At first I thought it was a rhetorical question. But I've given this come-on a brief reprieve for a simple reason: it worked.

"*I know I should have told you this before, but I have a boyfriend.*"

This is not the sort of thing that just slips your mind for the night. It's not that I never want to hear this; I just prefer to receive information on a need-to-know basis. A good time would be when the boyfriend appears and begins beating on the door to the bathroom stall. If there is not imminent danger, keep it to yourself. It makes the absolution of guilt much easier for me.

Although each of the above phrases will always work my last queer nerve, two phrases remain that never fail to strike terror into my heart: "*I'll call you*" and "*I love you.*"

Yeah, right.

Meet the 'Rents

The whole gay marriage issue has brought up a number of questions in my mind. For instance, if I decide to get married, we'll both be grooms. Since weddings have traditionally been paid for by the bride's family, which family can we scam into paying for the event which, of course, would be a large and stunning affair?

And, considering tradition once again, which of the grooms' fathers must be asked for permission to take his son's hand in marriage? Or would I ask his mother? Or must there be a joint consensus of both families, second cousins included?

This seems like an awful lot of trouble to go to for a blender and microwave. *

I suppose I'm getting somewhat ahead of myself, given that marriage doesn't seem to be an imminent prospect

---

* Now that I'm actually all grown up and married, I can attest that it *is* a lot of trouble to go through for a blender and microwave (and a full set of china). But it's worth it.

for me. More relevant to my situation is how to handle the introduction of a boyfriend.

For years I had to listen to all the news of my sister's latest boyfriends while any mention of my romantic life was conspicuously absent. In time I became jealous, partly because my life was being ignored, but mostly because I didn't have a romantic life to talk about anyway.

When I finally did meet the man I considered Mr. Right, I gleefully told my parents, waxing on and on and on about how happy we were together and the life we intended to build together and what our common tastes in home decor were. All this was two weeks into the relationship. Two weeks later, we had broken up. It was years before I again mentioned a boyfriend to my parents. Embarrassment is a powerful thing.

My family actually met my first boyfriend, although they had no idea that "boyfriend" was how he should be viewed. They thought he was a nice boy who decided to spend his spring break in the backwoods of Fredonia with his fraternity brother instead of heading to Florida for sun and beer busts or Colorado for skiing and hot tubs.

Like, duh.

Funny thing is, my family loved him. Everyone from Granny on down thought he was the nicest, sweetest thing. I did too, though in a completely different context. I had the strangest feeling (later verified) that my teenage sister was developing a slight crush.

During this romantic spring break week, our goal was to have sex in every room of the house, as well as the railroad trestle in the field out back. Hey, we were eighteen—we had the stamina back then. We had almost succeeded when one afternoon, as I stood there with a large glob of freshly-applied Vaseline slathered all over one of my body parts and him naked on the living room floor, I heard a car pull into the driveway. The one time in my life that my family would come home early from shopping at the Paducah Mall, and they picked that afternoon.

I suppose pickings were slim at the Piggly Wiggly.

The other advantage of being eighteen was having the speed of mind and body to get cleaned up and dressed before they even opened the front door.

When it comes to parents, I can only offer one piece of wisdom: don't use nicknames for your boyfriend in front of your parents. I'm sure your mother doesn't want to know that you call him "Tastybutt."

You Want Fries With That?

W hen you mention sex and food in the same sentence, most people think of the simple admonishment not to go out for Mexican with your new boyfriend if you intend to have an intense roll in the hay later that night (and if you do, stop by CVS first to invest in some breath mints and Massengill).

But aside from those words of wisdom and experience, food and sex can mix quite well. I'm surprised the makers of Cool Whip haven't developed an additional product line for sale at outlets such as the Leather Rack.

Many sex-oriented shops already stock what appears to be foodstuff—although the nutritional value of these materials must be somewhere below that of "processed cheese-food," and I don't consider flavored oils and edible panties to be a good substitute for what I can find in my own pantry.

Many people consider bringing items of food into sex to spice up a relationship, hence all the giggling male couples you see at the Soviet Safeway shopping for cucumbers, eggplants, and (for relationships seriously foundering on the rocks) watermelons. What they don't realize is that food can be the last-minute item that saves a sexual encounter from becoming a night of disappointment.

One evening, back during my more adventurous youth (when stimulation by beverages and other chemicals was a much higher priority), I brought home a self-professed aggressive, military bottom. This man made no bones about his desires—from the time I met him by the dance floor till I brought him through the front door, all I heard was that he wanted me to drive his highway.

For a guy who's always assumed to be a complete bottom, this was pretty ego-building stuff (I was too new in town at the time to realize how desperate a bottom can get).

So I have this guy lying on my bed, his knees where his epaulets would be, and I can't get my willie to even a three-quarter salute, much less enough stiffness to get to work on his foxhole.

Beyond the help of poppers and improvised cock rings, only one option came to my lust-ridden mind: run to the kitchen.

All I could find was a bottle of Log Cabin maple syrup, which, in the end, did the trick nicely. In fact, I found that the distinctive shape of the bottle facilitates some activities that probably never crossed the minds of the manufacturers. (I'll leave all jokes about ass-kissing and gay Republicans to you.)

Important safety tip to make me look more responsible: many items you find in your kitchen contain oils and other nasty little things that can cause your protective latex barriers to weaken and break. This is important because, although tasty on items other than pancakes, Log Cabin syrup does not contain a spermicide. Of course, using honey or chocolate syrup as a lubricant strikes me as a bit counter-productive.

Bon appétit!

The Seven Habits of
Highly Annoying People

As you pass your time idly thumbing through the pages of *Vanity Fair* or *People*, you may ask yourself, "Am I annoying enough?" After all, the world seems filled with those who have an abundance of annoying tendencies, whether within the glossy pages of a magazine, on the *Ricki Lake* soundstage, in congressional hearings on homosexuality, or against the rail at your neighborhood bar.

To help you catch up, here are the seven basic steps to annoying behavior.

Number 1: Don't worry about paying for cocktails— that's what friends are for. If they expect you to take time out of your busy schedule to socialize with them, they should make some sort of offering. As a corollary, don't buy cigarettes either. Remember, the more of your friends' cigarettes you smoke, the less likely they are to die of lung cancer.

Number 2: Never commit. If someone invites you over for dinner, simply say "That sounds good. I'll call you tomorrow." Leave yourself open should a better opportunity arise. And who cares if your friend has to turn down offers of dinner, drinks, and dates? It's his fault for being so rigid.

Number 3: Take a cue from my grandmother's handbook: if you can't talk about it before 10:00 AM, it's not worth talking about. So what if it's Sunday? You haven't been to bed yet, but you still have the energy to call. Surely your sleeping friend can muster the energy to listen to your exploits from the night before. If you want, make your friend talk with the boy lying next to you in bed—it's always rude not to make prompt introductions.

Number 4: Whenever you visit someone's home, be sure to leave some important personal item behind. However, don't call to ask for its retrieval until you need it right then. Preferably, this will be when the homeowner in question is walking out the door for his two-week European vacation. Make promises you can't keep about getting him to the airport. Remember, the more drama the better.

Number 5: Make cocktail parties more interesting by always being the last to laugh at a joke—but be sure to make your laugh as insincere and condescending as possible, so everyone will know that you, of course, were among the first to spread that joke about O.J. and Michael Jackson on the golf course with Lisa Marie in the sand trap.

Number 6: Fashionably late is passé—it only applies to cocktail parties and nightclubs. Instead, concentrate on being late for every conceivable event, including family meals, commitment ceremonies, business meetings, and driving your best friend to the emergency room. The more time they spend waiting on you, the more time they will have for some much-needed reflection about why they are not as fabulous as you.

Number 7: Always claim that you're not annoying. "Whatever could have made you say that?"

As you may have guessed, this one is my personal favorite.

Move Along, Little Doggie

You know those evenings when you go out with friends to one of the more popular nightspots in town, only to find yourself crushed against the bar by the relentless and never ebbing swell of the crowd until you feel your only option is to jump atop the bar and scream, "*Soylent Green is people!*"

I know them well. In fact, I've been out on so many such trips I can hardly keep track. Although, to be honest, I tend to scream something along the lines of, "*Someone take me home right now!*"

When I was somewhat younger, I thought it quite fun to wander through the impacted masses of the gay bar crowd, where it took at least thirty minutes to get to the bathroom, not counting the time spent in line to actually visit a stall. Of course, the line for the women's room is usually much longer and, consequently, much more fun.

But that is not today's topic.

Now that I find myself somewhat older and working a job that doesn't pay overtime, I've become somewhat discontent with crowded bars. I say "somewhat" because my content or discontent with a crowded bar depends, naturally, upon the conduct of the crowd itself.

As you may have guessed by this point, I'm tired of being shoved around in a crowded bar by pushy queens.

I understand that when you can get a dollar cocktail, some social norms tend to go out the window. I even understand someone entering a frenzy because, by taking off his shirt and showing his flabby and dangling pecs, a free drink is proffered by the bartender.

I cannot, however, understand those people who shove me against a wall in order to speed their own trip to the bar. I mean, Jesus! What is their rush? It's not like they're in the former Soviet Union or something, where getting a vodka tonic depends on how fast the bartender can squeeze and ferment potatoes.

In my mind (which may be a tenuous thing at best, but that's beside the point), going out with friends should be a relaxing experience. In effect, I should not have to find myself suffering a ruptured appendix as the result of an Oompa-Loompa-on-steroids crashing through the crowd to find a diet-drug supplier who happens to be stocked for the evening.

A bar is not a racetrack. If the gorgeous man you flirt with on the other side of the club can't wait five minutes for you to slog your way through your bar brethren, then it's not worth it. Should someone else beat you to him, who cares? If this one man was your only chance at happiness, perhaps your time would be better spent in an overly darkened sex club than in a bar.

There are words appropriate to use should you find yourself having to adopt a more forceful manner in your travels. Perhaps you've heard of them: "Excuse me," "Pardon me," "I'm so sorry, let me buy you another one."

Strive to be polite as you crash through throngs of tipsy boys. Remember, in a crowd, it may be hard to tell exactly who kicked your clumsy feet out from underneath you.

Cry Me a River

Add yet another item to the list of reasons to be jealous of women: they get to cry.

I don't mean that women cry all the time, or even that every time they cry it's completely accepted. I remember the Pat Schroeder incident, but politicians get attacked for how many times a day they go to the bathroom, so that's a different story.

But in the real world, where I spend about half of my time, things are different. Women are allowed to cry. Men aren't.

Since most of us gay men were sissy boys of one kind or another while growing up (even if you claim to be one of those straight-acting, macho fags, we know you tried on your mother's high heels a few times, too), we learned pretty early what made you a sissy: reading too much, getting whacked upside the head in dodge ball, and crying.

When I made the connection that the more I cried the more I would get whacked upside the head in PE,

I learned not to cry in front of or within five miles of anyone else.

My experiences with women friends have taught me that crying can be an effective release of tension. A few have told me that, in the middle of a particularly frustrating day at work, they will go to a bathroom stall, cry a bit, and then come back to their desk able to face the tyrannical boss once again.

If a man tries that, all he'll hear is vicious snickering from the urinals. Most likely he would come back to his desk to find a giant box of Puffs in his chair. If you are a man working in the corporate world, your reputation will be far more damaged by a semi-public crying jag than, say, having your boss find you sucking off a bike courier in a stairwell.

Having been told so many times that boys don't cry, I've learned a number of techniques to hold back the flow. Particularly effective is biting my tongue until it bleeds, somewhat similar to how I keep from laughing out loud at death scenes in movies like *Beaches* and *Steel Magnolias*. But that doesn't work well when you're talking to someone who's making you want to cry, like your ex-boyfriend or parole officer.

A friend told me that not crying is like not puking— you fight both of them off for as long as you can, but you feel a lot better when you're through. Given the near superhuman effort I put into the avoidance of both crying and puking, it comes as no surprise that when I finally get around to doing either, it's pretty damn loud.

I lost my crying control at a nightclub one evening a few years back, after being fired from a shit job earlier in the day (a few pitchers of beer loosened me up). As I sat out on the patio being comforted by friends, I thought I would never live down the embarrassment of the moment.

Fortunately, a big-haired suburban chick chose that moment to divert the crowd's attention from me by performing a power puke on the dance floor.

She should have had more self control.

Warning Signs

Perhaps one of the most important skills you can have as a gay man is the ability to make decisions about your love life based on observing the object of your affections and his surroundings. That's why I continue to develop my catalog of warning signs that tell me, "Run! Run for your life!"

Use these guidelines at your own risk—I make no guarantees.

No Books.

I managed to remain a voracious reader even after the tons of abuse I received in elementary school for being a bookworm. Given that, it's unlikely I will cut down on my reading at this point in my life.

It's depressing to walk into some cute guy's apartment and realize the only reading material to be found is the Chinese takeout menu hanging on the fridge. What does he do with his time? Watch *Nick at Night*?

An even more egregious transgression is a lack of reading material in the bathroom. Trust me, I've already read the back of every hygienic product made in this country. Is it too much to ask for a copy of *Time* or *Newsweek*? I'd even settle for *People* in a pinch.

I once had a boyfriend who asked me, in all seriousness, "Why do you read so much?" Of course, he thought *Shining Time Station* was a pretty cool show.

The relationship ended shortly thereafter.

Bad Books.

To return to the bathroom for a moment, there are inappropriate reading materials. For example, porno mags are not a good thing. For those of us who sport a certain angle in our tumescence, sexually stimulating materials can make a trip to the bathroom a bit problematic. Try standing on your head to pee sometime and you'll see what I mean.

Religious books are not necessarily a bad sign—even I have a few Bibles in my house, and I have a hard time remembering the difference between the altar and the sanctuary. However, if you find something like *Converting the Homosexual* and autographed photos of Fred Phelps and Pat Robertson, immediately jump through the nearest window.

Bedside books should also be evaluated. Gigantic tomes by Russian writers are appropriate due to their sleep-inducing characteristics. A copy of *Slice and Dice: The Beginner's Guide to Ritual Scarification* may tell you it's time to leave.

Hand Check.

You may have a problem if you realize the callous on your potential mate's index finger comes not from playing the cello but from popping tops from an ongoing bevy of beer bottles (bartenders have an excuse). If the callous comes from his continual masturbation, you may have a problem of a different sort, depending on what your sex drive is for that lunar cycle.

Be careful not to assume a callous is always a bad thing. These days, calloused hands are about the only way to tell the difference between people who do real physical work and us white-collar types who would be right at home in *Dilbert*.

But in the interest of your own genital comfort, make sure that your calloused partner always has a lot of lube on hand.

Surviving the Season

Until this Thanksgiving, I had never taken home a boyfriend to meet my family—at least officially. When I was in college I brought home a friend who was more than a friend, and my family remained blissfully ignorant of the true nature of the relationship. Of course, we broke up soon thereafter, making it all the more difficult over the next four years to answer the incessant question, "He was so nice, when is he coming back for another visit?"

Granny, if you only knew.

This time, however, was different. By choosing to come out to one of my cousins, who conveniently served as the biggest family gossip, I had announced my queerness to every Bugg within the continental United States, with the exception of my grandfather. Being nearly deaf, he was left to figure it out on his own.

"Sean's kind of strange," he told my sister, in one of my favorite understatements of the year. "I guess he doesn't like girls very much."

Even though everyone finally had confirmation on my "strangeness," that doesn't mean that everyone likes it. I've gotten a couple of letters from Granny on the subject; I've dubbed them the "Devil Letters."

You can see why I was a bit nervous bringing home a boyfriend to sit down for dinner with my extended family in the presence of a carving knife and other utensils. Hell, I get nervous just crossing the District line into Virginia.

But I learned two important lessons on this trip home, which I think may benefit anyone out there preparing to take the same familial leap.

Number One: Don't underestimate your family.

Expecting the worst, I found myself in shock when southern hospitality outweighed religious objections to queers. When my boyfriend made an offhand comment about how much he liked the raw turnips, Granny took mere seconds to peel and slice a new turnip just for him.

Given Granny's propensity for cornering people for one-on-one discussions of faith, I kept a close eye on her and my boyfriend the whole day. At one point, I spotted her alone with him by his car. Fearing the worst, I rushed over to save him.

Much to my chagrin, it turned out they were bonding over driving tips. While I was touched by Granny's acceptance of his presence, I can only hope he doesn't actually implement any of her tips. [Granny's rule for backing up: place car in reverse and press accelerator. Repeat process until all cars have been cleared from path.]

It all kind of made me glad for my small-town upbringing.

Number Two: Don't overestimate your family.

If you plan to bring a partner home for the first time, you absolutely must do one of two things—either work out the sleeping arrangements before you ever leave your own house or make hotel reservations.

If you find separate bedrooms (as I did), don't bother raising a fuss. You don't want to piss off your parents at the start of the Christmas shopping season. Haven't you ever noticed that couples tend to get better gifts than singles?

Happy pragmatic holidays!

Hurry Up!

S calia. Sca - *li* - a.

Sort of rolls off the tongue, doesn't it? Did you notice that "Scalia" and "scat" begin with the same three letters? Coincidence?

I think not.

These are the types of things I come up with when I start pondering. Obviously, I shouldn't ponder so much, but I just can't stop, even when hair sprouts on my palms.

Just last night I was playing with my roommate's dog, and I decided it would be fun to do the "dog thing"—scratching his hindquarters until his leg starts doing that uncontrollable scratching movement. (I suppose I should get out more, but that's beside the point at the moment.)

After about ten minutes or so of this, the dog's leg still hadn't started twitching. There were a couple of moments when it seemed to be close, but then it didn't happen. It was then, as my arm began to cramp from continuous scratching, that I realized the similarity between this situation and some of the men in my past.

Who hasn't found themselves in bed with a man who can't make it past the finish line, but refuses to take a rain check? (Note: lesbians are not required to answer that question.) At times I've found myself pumping and pumping and pumping until I become delusional, thinking I'm Annie Sullivan, and screaming "Goddammit Helen, it's water! It's water!"

I would like to propose a simple etiquette rule for all those men out there who occasionally find that nirvana is out of reach for the moment, which, I believe, includes everyone. If your helpful partner has switched hands more than four times, he's probably getting tired and you should offer to take over.

Orgasmic delay can also be a problem outside of digital stimulation. On one of those rare nights when you're a bottom and in the mood to do it, and you've found a top who's not too tweaked to do it, you may still find yourself frustrated.

Really, there are only so many ways I can position my pelvis, contract my muscles and grunt phrases I would never say in the light of day. Beyond that, there's not a whole lot I can do. One night, about thirty minutes after I had come out of pure frustration, my partner finally decided to take control, barking "On your back! On your stomach! On all fours! On the stove!"

I thought I had stumbled into a Jane Fonda workout video, though I suppose *Buns of Steel* would be more appropriate.

Don't get me wrong. I don't think sex should be a sixty-second affair (with a few public exceptions), but it shouldn't be an iron man competition either. Although it's a laudable goal to bring both yourself and your partner across the finish line, an orgasm is not required. This is particularly true when your partner is someone you've only recently met.

So please have mercy on our poor bodies when you realize the time will not come, give us a little kiss, and hold us gently while we sleep through the morning and into the early afternoon.

Just be ready to try again when you wake up.

Camille Paglia Takes Over

I'm not a big believer in New Age mumbo jumbo. In fact, I think The Celestine Prophecy *has a good chance of winning the prize of worst book of the twentieth century. However, as a big fan of Camille Paglia, I have to tell you a spooky story that makes more sense than the healing aura of the surrounding flora. After being turned on to Paglia by a friend, I found myself ripping through* Sexual Personae; Sex, Art and American Culture; *and even the self-promoting* Vamps and Tramps, *loving every word she put to paper. Enamored as I was, one evening I dreamed that I had the opportunity to interview my prickly heroine. The very next morning, my editor called to offer me the opportunity to interview Paglia and her lover, Allison Maddox—the couple were in town promoting a new microbrewery. Not surprisingly, Paglia wasn't happy with my interview and the magazine office received one of her patented voice mail messages, including her outrage that we completely ignored Allison during the course of the interview. I think the rest of this column explains itself.*

A little lesbianism goes a long way.

Which is why, of course, the editors of *Metro Weekly* have invited me to contribute on occasion to "The Back Room," given my long experience writing brilliantly incisive social criticism in my *Advocate* column. Although I suspect it also has something to do with the usual columnist wanting some extra time off.

After reviewing Mr. Bugg's columns, I think taking some time off is wise. Until recently, I had thought the most boring way to spend a Sunday would be brunching with a group of Birkenstock-clad American lesbians at the local Pancake House. But after slogging through Bugg's bathos-masquerading-as-humor, I feel as if I've been force fed more sleeping pills than Marilyn Monroe.

I mean, come on.

It's always whine, whine, whine about not having a boyfriend, how the boyfriends he somehow snags always dump him, or his thoughts on the function of his different orifices. As I've always done in my best-selling work, including *Sexual Personae*, I've come up with a new term to describe this type of writing: anal gazing.

Get over it, Bugg! If I hadn't been forced to look at those pictures (which, by the way, have no redeeming artistic value according to the criteria delineated in my book *Sex, Art and American Culture*) I would have thought you were some middle-class, anorexic college girl misdirecting her energy from her sexual attraction to her father's third cousin, twice removed.

Speaking of so-called anorexic women, my lover and I have been developing a new form of art to combat this anti-pleasure attitude so prevalent among lesbians today. Honey, why don't you tell them about our new exhibit?

Well, Camille …

Exactly! Right, right! Lesbians just aren't any fun! I mean, you go to a lesbian club and what do they do? They sit around all night eating low-fat pretzels and drinking fizzy water. And don't even watch them on the dance floor. Terrible, terrible.

Of course, I adore gay men and they adore me. Tell them, honey.

Wherever we go …

Yes, yes! That's what I'm saying! It doesn't matter where we go—gay men just swarm all over me. It's amazing how I can instantly start having a conversation with a gay waiter, but the instant I start talking to some uptight lesbian, she just turns off.

I think there may be a reason for …

Yeah, right! Gay men are so full of life, just like those working class people you find out in the Midwest. They enjoy what life has to offer, they yell, they drink, they live with abandon. Of course, sometimes the working class people will go, you know, beat the hell out of some fags, but I think the comparison holds.

But …

But people don't like to listen to the working class, exactly right! That's why so many of those Steinem feminists and Foucault fags don't want to listen to me.

I'm an Italian! We say what we mean. Like "penis envy." Yeah, penis envy. I've got it, you've got it, all women have it. They just don't want to hear about it.

I'm outta here …

Exactly!

Extra Meat

While I've never gone overboard about it, I've always harbored a certain fascination with uncircumcised penises. Having gone under the knife at birth myself, I suppose this has something to do with wanting what I don't have.

Plus, finding out your friend has a little extra meat can often add to the fun of an evening. Not everyone agrees with me on this, however. An older friend of mine professes to profound disgust with the presence of foreskin. He refuses to believe the arguments of myself and others that, when the member he maligns rises to the occasion, it's pretty hard to even tell the difference (with the exception of the stars of Kristen Bjorn's Brazilian-based porno films, but guys who can masturbate without touching themselves are in a different category anyway).

I've made other arguments on behalf of the natural penile sheath that have also gone unheeded, particularly that late twentieth-century advances in personal hygiene technology and habits have made it possible to present a foreskin without a side dish of crackers (unless, of course, that happens to be your thing).

But my friend continues to voice his disgust for any turtle-neck equipped trouser snake. I suppose this is why, rather than celebrate Christmas, he chooses to celebrate the day of the Holy Circumcision, which, not surprisingly, falls during the early days of January. Each year, in honor of the occasion, I receive a holiday card—and you can guess what the picture is.

My friend has mentioned at times that the remains of the Holy Circumcision, or the Holy Foreskin, I suppose, are still in existence, which makes me believe the Church will hang onto anything. I mean, by this point I'm sure the thing looks like a dehydrated jalapeno. What if some practical jokester bishop put it on the pope's pizza?

Just a thought.

At the other end of the spectrum are those men who will do anything, go to any lengths, to get their foreskins back. I first heard of foreskin restoration techniques while in college, although I decided to save my foray into cosmetic surgery for a time when I really need it. Say, next year or so. Anyway, in my own little effort to help the fledgling movement, I ran a public service announcement in the student newspaper: "Lost part of your best friend? Call 1-800-FOR-SKIN."

I'm not sure if they got any calls.

What bothers me is the techniques used for the rebirth of the foreskin. After suffering as a small child through the experience of having it sliced off, do I really want to have another portion of my body sliced off and attached to the end of my penis? Or have weights attached to stretch what little skin the doctors left behind? I would feel like my dick had suddenly become the property of Dr. Frankenstein or Charles Atlas.

I think that all the men out there who want to reclaim the personal property they lost at birth should make a pilgrimage to Rome and kiss the Holy Foreskin. At least it wouldn't hurt.

Divine Comedy

According to all the lessons I learned in Sunday school (at least those I remember), one cannot prove that God exists. You must have faith and believe. Personally, I believe that this doctrine should be taught in introductory public relations classes as the first example of "spinning" an issue.

Anyway, it's not the existence of God that concerns me. I'm concerned with proving that God, if he/she/it exists, has a sense of humor. For proof of this hypothesis, one has to look no further than between one's own legs.

Can you think of any other reason a deity would make our sexual organs double as excretory organs? Think about it. If Athena had designed the human functions of sex and expurgation, they would have each been distinct (and most likely self-cleansing). If Dionysus, the god of good wine, orgies, and really good parties, had drawn up the blueprints, our bodies would be covered with extra gonads.

But no. God decided it would be much funnier to see men with erections trying to pee into toilets.

Our eyes don't have to bear this burden of double duty. And what do our ears do, besides hear? (Producing unsightly ear wax and hairs doesn't count as a legitimate function.) I suppose the nose carries out a number of functions, but outside of breathing, many of those functions are illegal in the fifty states and territories.

I believe God also gets a kick out of watching all the fundies get worked up about those "dirty, filthy" things we queers do with our part-time excretory organs. Remember, some of these fundies have claimed that all gay men eat approximately six pounds of fecal matter a year. Sounds to me like a few people must be going back for seconds, thirds, and fourths at a particularly bizarre buffet table. It's as if these fundies have never heard of enemas and toilet paper. Which could, of course, be the case.

Another piece of evidence of the existence of God's humor can be summed up in three words: Pat Robertson lives.

For those of you who remember bible school, think back to what happens to all those people God loves.

They get sold into slavery by their brothers. They wander the desert for forty years. They turn into pillars of salt. They're afflicted by boils and pestilence. Children of the righteous get their hair caught in trees and die.

And if God truly, deeply loves you with whipped cream and a cherry on top, you get nailed to a big piece of wood.

Contrast this with people God didn't like. The Egyptians got some frogs dropped on them, but otherwise did quite well after God showed the Hebrews the exit to the desert. It seems to me that most everyone in the bible who should be seen as wicked possesses amazing amounts of money and gold extorted from a nearly enslaved populace.

Pat Robertson is quite rich. He's adored by millions who send him checks. You can do the math.

That God. What a joker.

Nic Fit

I've been thinking lately that I want to get some.

No, I'm not talking about sex, for once. I've already got that. What I'm talking about are all those billions of dollars the tobacco industry wants to put into a fund to pay off smokers. Hey, it's the American way.

By way of background, I first started smoking at sixteen, primarily because I thought smoking a Camel while driving a 1976 Firebird looked pretty cool. I say "first" because I quit sometime after I turned seventeen, just before I went to college. I quit by employing a time-honored tactic—chain smoking an entire pack until I puked.

Obviously, this technique works best before you move up to three packs a day.

During my freshman year of college, I picked up the habit once again. Being a shy and nervous person at parties (no, really, I am), I needed something to do with my hands that wouldn't frighten my fraternity brothers.

Occasionally holding my cigarette in Bette Davis fashion might have given them a few hints, but I don't think any of them had seen *All About Eve*.

At the time, I claimed I took up smoking because one night I happened to watch *St. Elmo's Fire*, the brat pack stars of which spent more time smoking than acting. I'm not sure what I'm more ashamed of—that I again picked up a habit that yellowed my teeth, made my clothes stink, and shortened my life span, or that I once found Andrew McCarthy really hot.

In truth, I just started smoking again because I liked it and I wanted to, not because the media made me do it. But that reason's not going to win me any lawsuits, so I'm going to stick to my original story.

I've been a smoker for more than a decade. I've changed my brand from Camel Lights to Marlboro Lights, in spite of the fact that I happen to like Camel's amusingly phallic mascot. Smoking Camels has the unfortunate side effect of making my gums bleed. I doubt that particular benefit will be mentioned in any Camel advertisements in the near future, unless the FDA gets their way (they could get Mel Brooks to direct the commercials: "Emphysema, here we go! Emphysema, my lungs can't blow!").

But, while I've never found myself attracted to the Marlboro Man, I do like the fact that if I smoke like a fiend for another five years or so, I can get a free leather jacket.

Unfortunately, those five years of smoking are part of the problem. I've noticed that the only people suing the tobacco companies are smokers who have to be wheeled into the courtroom in an iron lung or some other elaborate medical equipment impressive to juries. I mean, sure, a couple million would help pay the medical bills, but what else can you do with it at that point? It's a bit late by then to be investing in fancy beach houses and flashy sports cars.

So, in the best interests of everyone, the tobacco companies should cough up the dough for me now, before I have to cough up a lung.

Bed Head

I've heard, as I'm sure you have, that the average person spends about one-third of his life sleeping. Combine this with the amount of time you spend having sex, either with a partner or your favorite hand, and you can see why beds play such an important role as a foundation of our society.

Given this, I've found it interesting to determine what beds can say about their owners, particularly when said owner is a potential mate. Of course, you don't need me to tell you what it means when you walk into a man's bedroom to find a frilly canopy bed straight out of Barbie's Dream House (but just in case you do need to know, it means trouble).

Instead, in stereotypical fashion, I'm more concerned with the size.

The Twin.

After a night of trying to fit into one of these with a friend, your body will be so cramped and twisted that you won't be able to make it to the bathroom, much less disentangle your limbs from his. On the bright side, you will be qualified to audition for Andrew Lloyd Webber's next musical, based on *The Hunchback of Notre Dame: Hump!*, featuring the sure-to-be hit, "I've Got a Hunch About You."

Do yourself a favor and just sleep on the floor—that's where you'll end up anyway.

The Foreign.

Not so long ago, I owned a platform bed that was bigger than a twin but smaller than a full. I always referred to it as "European size," which was appropriate given that it was no more than a twin with a snotty attitude.

Also included in this category are the ubiquitous futons. It's hard for me to take seriously a bed that sounds like a band name. Though I have to admit the name does lend itself to jokes: one friend of mine dubbed a certain notorious futon, the scene of much boinking I'd rather not think about, the "poopton."

You figure it out.

Full Size.

This is the boy-next-door of the bed kingdom. It's big enough for two, but doesn't make single boys feel lonely. I've found that many full-sized owners are the younger, career-minded gay boys who've shown they are responsible enough to move beyond the realm of twins and futons and into the world of real beds.

Of course, you may find out he picked it up from an eviction pile on Sixteenth Street, in which case he's just a scumbag.

The Queen.

In addition to having the best name, this one has the most practical size. Unlike the full size, you can find a little bit of space away from your bed-hogging partner. And unlike the king size, you and your partner can actually sleep in the same Zip code.

The King.

When it comes to beds, the king size is the Jaguar—a product that allows a man to pretend his dick is bigger than it really is. But as long as your potential mate isn't in too much need of psychological support concerning his crotch, take this size while you can get it.

Think of the king size as one of those huge, impossible looking dildos: you'll never be able to use every inch of it, but it's comforting to know you have them.

Back Off

For some unknown reason, it seems I've gotten a reputation for being a cynical bastard who doesn't like people. That is just so wrong. I love people. My love for people makes the world go 'round. It's just all the idiots I don't like.

And it's not my fault there are so damn many of them running around loose out there. I swear there must be an idiot farm somewhere near DC, most likely in Manassas.

Interestingly enough, most of the idiots who try to interrupt the calm, peaceful nature of my life do so while I'm somewhere near my office. And one of the most notorious of these idiots is the "Anti-Smoking Busybody."

Now, before some anti-smoking group sends a black, windowless van to my home, I'm not saying that all anti-smoking people are idiots. Smoking is a vile habit that makes you smell bad and die young. Everyone who smokes should stop now. Or maybe tomorrow.

Anyway, as a conscientious member of humanity and an avid fan of Miss Manners, I've dutifully followed all the rules on smoking. When I get the urge for nicotine, I join the mob of other smokers out on the sidewalk, where we fight for space with the homeless folks. At restaurants, I always sit well within the smoking section. I have no desire to inflict my habit on others.

But one morning as I came out of the Metro, a woman followed me so closely that I thought I would have to use toilet paper to get her off. Even in the morning rush hour there's plenty of room for people to move along the sidewalk without attaching themselves to me. Of course, I went on with my usual routine of lighting a cigarette approximately four steps away from the escalator.

My new Siamese twin was not amused, and huffed something about smokers that I couldn't quite make out, but that I assume was not pleasant. Poor little thing. But situations like this are the reason God gave us lungs to blow smoke into the faces of others.

You may have deduced by now that most of the people I consider to be idiots have in some way violated my personal space, to which I can only say, "You betcha!" I'm not that partial to being touched or crowded by people I consider my friends, much less a bunch of strangers on an elevator. Why, when I'm one of two passengers in an elevator, does the other person insist on standing right behind me? Or, even worse, try to start a conversation with me?

And speaking of elevators and talking, I'm sure many of you office workers out there would agree with me that those idiots who hold open an elevator door to continue a conversation with someone *outside* the elevator should be lined up on the loading dock and forced to smell the dumpster for an hour.

I think the world of office buildings would be a much more pleasant place if elevators came equipped with a panic button for the use of passengers when some idiot is delaying the trip this way. When pressed, sharp needles would spring from the door edges, thereby speeding the trip.

Although I think the more civilized solution would be to just let me smoke at my desk so I wouldn't have to be out among the people quite so often.

"Macbeth! Macbeth!"

Contrary to stereotype, I've never found myself particularly interested in theater. You can probably tell this because I spell theater the correct, American way, and not the frou-frou, British "theatre." As if switching two letters at the end of a word would distract me from noticing that the talent behind the creation of, say, *Cats* is somewhere along the lines of an Ed Wood movie.

There are some theatrical productions that I've enjoyed. I've been a fan of Shakespeare ever since my high school English teacher took me to a production of *All's Well That Ends Well*. And, as you might expect, I tend to enjoy plays that involve nudity (which most of Shakespeare's plays could use during Act IV).

But when it comes to musical theater, I couldn't care less. In fact, I'd rather sit through another Marilyn Manson show than one of these touring Broadway "blockbusters" that hit DC with more frequency than protest marches.

It's not that I haven't tried to enjoy them or don't understand the work that goes into them. I just don't like the music. This may be the result of growing up as a heavy-metal head. Hey, I don't like Madonna either.

[Just as an aside, the funniest thing I've seen on television was a woman complaining as she came out of the Madonna movie version of *Evita*. "I wish there had been more dialogue," she said. What was she expecting? *My Dinner with Andre*? *The Conversation*? I may not like musicals, but at least I understand that they contain music.]

I suppose this makes me a member of the target audience for "rock operas." Unfortunately for the producers of these shows, I find them even sillier than *Bye, Bye Birdie*.

For example, when I watched the movie version of *Hair!* I found myself wanting to yell, "Get a damn job!" I have little patience for watching a bunch of do-gooder hippies dance around a park thinking they're making the world a better place. Go do another tab, Moonbeam, and call me next century.

When I went to see *Tommy*, I found that the show had been somewhat sanitized from the original, presumably so the Boomers could bring their kids and save money on babysitting.

I was going to mention *Rent*, but given that I may find a lynch mob at my front door if I do, I'll leave that one for sometime in the far, far future.

There's only one musical I've ever truly wanted to make a trip to New York to see: Stephen King's *Carrie*. I was surprised to find that even Broadway has some limits, and that particular show closed down approximately ten minutes after the curtain rose. Personally, in the age of special effects theater (what else can explain a Broadway show about the sinking of the Titanic?), I think *Carrie* was just a little ahead of its time. As a result, I'm still keeping my fingers crossed for a version of *Nightmare on Elm Street* (featuring the hit song, "Slicin' and Dicin'").

Or, even better, *Pink Flamingos*.

Out Done

Among the many bad habits in which I continue to indulge is the constant use of taxis. As a resident of one of DC's "transitional" neighborhoods, I have no nearby subway station, which means my public transportation options consist of rail-to-bus and bus-to-rail transfers complicated enough to give me a headache.

So the two-zone rush hour cab ride continues to be attractive to me.

The only problem with taking cabs is the possibility—make that the certainty—the cab driver will attempt to start a conversation. I've developed a number of defenses against this, most of which involve reading newspapers or other large pieces of paper that form a barrier between myself and the driver.

There are those drivers, however, who are undaunted by my silence. In these cases, I'm generally subjected to long-winded monologues about the Redskins or whatever testosterone-induced sport happens to be in season. Then, when I finally make the point that I don't watch or care about sports (with the exception of men's gymnastics, of course), I'm greeted with a disdainful snort.

Like he's going to care about any of my personal hobbies.

Sometimes the "conversation" drifts toward the other subject that seems to interest cabdrivers: breasts (also known as "ta-tas").

Last week during my cab ride home, the cabdriver suddenly honked his horn. "Just look at the pair on her," he said, turning his head toward me. "When they stand at attention like that you just have to salute, don't you think?"

This is where I know I should have said something like, "I prefer my ta-tas with a ding-dong," or something silly and off the cuff to let the lecherous driver know that women aren't my thing when it comes to, well, being a lech.

Instead, I merely smiled, nodded, and looked back to my paper. This made me realize an important fact: I'm sick to death of having to come out over and over and over again.

One of the great annoyances in life is the heterosexual presumption that I'm one of them, a presumption that still surprises me given the fact that I think I'm a big old queer. For all the blather that straights spout about being able to spot the fag, they sure seem to have a hard time when the genuine article is right in front of them.

Now, before anyone misunderstands, I think it's everyone's responsibility to get the hell out of the closet and come out in daily situations. You know, all that gaining our rights stuff. But for those of us who've been out for years, and on top of that make part of our living by being identified as gay, it gets a little tiring.

My dream is to have five minutes of time on all the major broadcast and cable networks so I can tell the country, once and for all, that I am a pansy, a fairy, a queer. Or, in the words of Marge Simpson, a "Ho! Mo! Sexual!"

Probably still wouldn't get the cab drivers to shut up.

Sporting Nuts

I am not a team player. Consequently, team sports have never played a central role in my life.

Don't forget—I grew up back before soccer became a female voting bloc, and, in those days, those who played it were all sissies with funny accents, so I never had the opportunity to discover what a wonderful, team-building experience this imported sport could be.

Instead, I managed to get sucked into Little League baseball. With a small portion of the genetic talent for softball from my mother's side of the family (most of my aunts and uncles could take your head off with a throw to first base), it was a successful attempt on my part to lower my sissy quotient by a few points.

This lasted for a few short seasons, after which I moved up to Pony League (and no, I have no idea why it was called "pony league," and I'm not even sure I could hazard a guess). At the end of my first pony season, I was named the only Fredonia representative on the county all-star team.

This was an excruciating experience because I was on a team with boys who, first of all, were far better players than I, and, secondly, didn't care for me much because I was from Fredonia (a sort of geographical sissy factor). Both of these assumptions appeared to be proven true when, on my first and only time on the field, I let a simple grounder go under my glove and between my feet.

It should come as no surprise that after this one season I gave up all future participation in team sports for the wonderful one-on-one world of tennis and racquetball.

I suppose I was conditioned to have a bad experience with team sports through my somewhat laughable attempts at participation in elementary school. Going out for a game of kickball or basketball or football during recess meant one thing to me: being picked last.

Back then nobody gave a damn about self-esteem and all that, so there was no program to ensure that at least once per month I got picked third or fourth to encourage my continued participation. As it was, I only got dragged into playing these games when my best friend Sammy Jack wasn't at school, meaning that we weren't off playing *Charlie's Angels*. (To this day I still harbor some resentment toward Kate Jackson because I always had to play the smart one, while Sammy Jack always got to be Farrah. Come to think of it, he always got to play Princess Leia, too, the little bastard.)

The only sport involving more than two people that I enjoyed playing in elementary school was "Smear the Queer." Obviously, this was before my political and personal enlightenment (although I hear it's still Pat Buchanan's favorite game).

To summarize, one boy grabs the ball (any sports-affiliated ball will do) and runs like hell to the safe zone at either end of the playing field. As you may have guessed, he's the "queer."

Meanwhile, ten to twenty other boys attempt to tackle the "queer," take possession of the ball, and run like hell for the safety zone. Fun is had by all, and play continues until a bone is broken or the playground monitor finally realizes what all the boys are up to.

I suppose it's true: everything I need to know about life I learned playing "Smear the Queer."

Out and About

My first true coming-out experience involved lots of running up and down the fire escape by my (then) fraternity brothers, much beating on my bedroom door, and a brief flirtation on my part with an eating disorder. As you may have guessed, it was more of an "outing" than a "coming out," and it wasn't a completely joyous experience, although it was a rather spectacular debut for me as an officially avowed homosexual.

Fortunately, we all have numerous coming-out events through the course of our lives, so if one gets royally screwed up—or a few—we can always hope for better the next time around. Say, perhaps, coming out to the parents.

On receiving the news, my mother stereotypically responded that she pretty much knew already. "You never dated in high school," she told me.

That particular circumstance was just as much a result of spending too much time running around getting drunk with my female classmates to actually date them as of my budding sexuality.

I never had a true coming-out moment with my father. My attempt at that came to center instead on the implication that my being gay had somehow played a role in my parents' divorce. Nothing like spreading around that familial responsibility.

After exiting the closet in front of one's parents, you have to do it all over again with the rest of the family. Never, ever assume that your parents are going to spread the news for you. Your parents will probably be the last ones to stop saying, "Oh, I'm sure he's still waiting to meet the right girl." Granny, on the other hand, has probably known since before your mother.

I cheated myself out of a big, dramatic coming-out spectacular with my extended family by taking the easy road out: I called the most gossipy of my cousins, and let her take it from there. This worked better than showing up at a family reunion in full drag with a half-naked gymbot on each arm ever could have.

Of all my various coming-out scenarios, few have actually approached the realm of high drama. Although, back when I was more stridently ideological, I firmly believed that the personal was the political. As such, I felt my personal life should be getting somewhat more of a political reaction, and I tended to look for those moments when my revelations would cause the biggest stir.

These days, not being quite so strident, I've come to the realization that the personal is personal, with the political as a sometimes-welcome secondary effect. Amazingly enough, this has provided me with more and more opportunities to come out.

When the person sitting next to me on the plane asks me if I'm married, I say yes—and I say how long my husband and I have been together.

When the bartender in a straight bar begins describing the woes of living with his girlfriend, such as pantyhose drying in the bathroom, I point out that living with another man presents an entirely different set of challenges.

And when some sweet old lady tells me about her wonderful grandchildren, I bring out the cutest possible stories about the darling little dogs who share my home.

The funny thing is, most of them keep listening.

Private Time

No matter how well you think you know someone, some things should remain private. For instance, certain bathroom functions.

Not everyone shares my view on this. We live in the Age of High Fiber in which discussion of bodily evacuations are almost as commonplace as chatting about the weather. Still, I have to ask everyone to please, please stop.

Perhaps I just have a fixation, but I've never been one to publicly flaunt my body's natural functions, either in conversation or in action. Well, some natural functions, but not that natural function.

Society expects men to be perfectly comfortable with this. Witness the lack of bathroom stall doors in high school and college dorm bathrooms. I could never completely adjust to those invasions of my privacy. During college, I devised convoluted schedules that would allow me at least five minutes alone to use the facilities.

Sitting on the toilet is my private time.

Things get no better with age. If I should find myself in need of private time in an office building, I can be sure that a busload of men will begin filing in and out of the restroom, similar to the way old people wait until you're on the road and running late for an important interview before turning on their left turn signal for three hundred miles or so.

Of course, I'm one of those people who will gladly pay the round-trip cab fare to home and back if that particular aspect of nature makes a call while I'm at work. And when it comes to sudden calls in bars and clubs, I think everyone should be willing to make that same sacrifice.

Living in the suburbs is no excuse. Think of it as another reason to move into the city.

Technology often plays a role in revealing a bit too much about people's private habits. I refer, of course, to those persons among us who insist on having telephone conversations while sitting on their personal thrones.

Listen closely: Alexander Graham Bell didn't mean it to be this way. You think he was sitting on the can when he yelled "Watson! Come here!"?

As Miss Manners points out so often, you are not required to answer the phone every time it rings. This is what the answering machine and voice mail are designed to do. Do not—I repeat, do not—take the phone into the bathroom.

But if you do, please don't let me know about it.

"Hey, what's up?"

"Oh, hi, Sean. I'm just sitting around."

"Cool. I just … wait, what's that splashing sound? Oh my god, you're not … *aaaauggghhhhh!*"

Click.

At the very least, you can lie and say you're washing the dishes.

Remember, talking on the phone while relaxing in a bubble bath with a glass of wine can be considered somewhat glamorous. Talking whilst perched on a porcelain potty will never be.

Snuggle Bunnies

A few years back, I remember reading the first of many Ann Landers columns in which women by the thousands wrote in to proclaim that they preferred "snuggling" and "cuddling" by far over the actual physical business of making whoopee.

At the time, my first thought was, *What the hell is up with that?* It seemed that women weren't from Venus but Pluto, or some point even further beyond. I mean, who wouldn't want to do the nasty?

And so went the thoughts of the twenty-four-year-old gay man set loose in the sexual candy store.

It's not really difficult to understand why I (and, I suspect, so many other men) thought this was yet another illustration of how women were so different. After all, I believed, my body didn't merely want sex, it required sex.

All this goes back to that moment experienced by virtually every boy nearing puberty—the erection that pops up in the five seconds before he's called to the blackboard. One of the great skills we men learn when young is how to hide an erect penis. Why else do you think so many boys like to wear their shirts untucked?

Those of us who are gay eventually have to unlearn these skills when we realize there are times when showing off can be advantageous—though not in some situations, such as your annual performance review with your boss (depending on the nature of your career).

When I was a teenager, I couldn't even put a book on my lap without popping a boner, which, given my status as an unremitting bookworm, was rather problematic. And it was difficult to get an even tan, since I had to spend all my time underwater while at the county pool—even a talented guy can't hide nature's desire in the confines of a Speedo.

One of the great cruelties of the world is the fact that men tend to reach their sexual peaks at around age nineteen. While this is fabulous for those in their late teens and early twenties, it can leave those on the bad side of the bell curve indulging in premature nostalgia.

Getting back to my point, all that sexual energy I had led to some interesting consequences. I had always envisioned the perfect relationship as one where sex happened, say, a couple times a day in various locations throughout the house.

The problem was that, while I expected to have just as much sex in a relationship as when I was single, I didn't realize that I didn't have as much sex as I thought I had when I was single. I couldn't have done so and still held down a job without some drastic changes to my career path.

So, now that I'm pushing thirty and in a relationship, I look at these preferences for cuddling and snuggling somewhat differently. While there's very little that surpasses the immediate intimacy of sex with the man I love, I feel better for longer when I'm just holding and being held.

Just as long as I don't have to call him "Pookie."

Yule Never Know

L EXINGTON, KY—At the risk of sounding like one of those New Age-ish, gay columnists looking for meaning in the belly-button lint of my life, I should point out that, as I write this, I've been thirty for just over eight hours.

(As an aside, I want to say thank-you to the alert reader who pointed out an error in a recent column about approaching age thirty; I'm actually entering my fourth decade of life, not my third. Thank you for catching my mistake. I really appreciate it. No, really.)

Actually, reaching my thirtieth birthday is somewhat anti-climactic. I knew that there would be no trumpets blaring from the sky to proclaim my ascension to a new level of life, but I did expect to feel somewhat different. Perhaps a sudden new perspective on life attainable only through experience.

Of course, I'm back home in Kentucky for Christmas, so I've already managed to gain a new perspective on life.

In fact, the number of new perspectives I've gained over the past few years of traveling home for the holidays may give me a kaleidoscope view.

Although I brought Mark home for Thanksgiving last year, this is the first time he has accompanied me for Christmas. My immediate family has taken a liking to him, and, after he cleaned my mom's kitchen while she was out visiting relatives, my mom probably likes him more than me on some levels.*

So Mark and I went down to my hometown to visit Granny and Grandpa a couple of days after Christmas, which allowed for a nice intimate visit without twenty or more extended family members asking us about Marion Barry.

Right after we walked in, Grandpa came over to me chuckling. He pointed at Mark and asked, "Is that your girlfriend?"

At that moment, I thought it would be the shortest visit ever to Granny's. I looked at Mark, whose jaw was somewhere near the couch. I was waiting for the other shoe to drop from Grandpa's mouth, but he just kept chuckling and shuffled off toward the kitchen.

Granny, of course, was in a complete tizzy after that, quickly telling us, "Don't listen to anything he has to say." As I went to help her make lunch (known as dinner in those parts, with supper to follow later, in case you're interested in those things), Grandpa pulled Mark aside.

---

*   Once the family took a liking to him, our days were numbered. Naturally, the break-up came not long after the holiday.

"It's just as good he doesn't have a girlfriend," Grandpa told him. "Those girls are just too much trouble to deal with these days."

In the country, when you reach ninety-four years old, you're pretty much allowed to say whatever you want. Just after that, Grandpa handed Mark a book of hillbilly jokes, instantly destroying all the hard work I had done breaking down stereotypes about Kentucky. Unfortunately, the best hillbilly jokes are told by the purported hillbillies themselves.

Later, Granny pulled me to the back of the house. Typically, this indicates a one-on-one mini-sermon about God and clean living, so I braced myself. She reached into a closet and pulled out a present.

"This is for you," she said, then hesitated for a moment. "And Mark."

I suppose new perspectives never stop coming.

This Is Only a Test

How many times have you heard that all gay men go through a second adolescence after leaving home and exploding out of the closet? And how many of you are tired of hearing this from straight people who have no earthly idea what they are talking about?

I thought so.

As a gay man who knows what he's talking about (at least some of the time), I've put together a quiz to determine whether you are or have been recapturing your teenage years during adulthood. Simply answer "Yes" or "No" to each of the following questions.

Question 1: Have you ever spent more than ten minutes in the ladies' room of a club for reasons having nothing to do with evacuation of your bladder or bowels?

Question 2: Have you ever shown up at someone's house at 5:00 AM on the barest hint of a whisper of a rumor that there might be a really hot after-hours party going on, only to find a groggy, pajama-clad man who wants more than anything to sleep?

Question 3: Have you, upon arriving at the above-mentioned home, managed to convince the resident to invite you and your friends in and throw open his bar?

Question 4: Have you ever uttered the following words, "I only did two small bumps, really. You should get that guy to check his scales."

Question 5: Have you ever walked out of a bar with your beer hidden under your coat? (Give yourself an extra point if you managed to escape successfully with a full cocktail.)

Question 6: Have you ever paid your rent late because you had to pay your recreational pharmaceuticals bill first? (Give yourself an extra point if you had to pay your mortgage late.)

Question 7: When calling in sick to work, have you ever forgotten that your office voice mail system includes a time stamp feature—and then realized you called at 3:00 AM?

Question 8: Have you ever taken a business trip to attend a very important meeting, only to miss the meeting because, when you emerged from your nightmare trick's apartment, you realized you were in a completely unfamiliar neighborhood with nary a taxicab in sight?

Question 9: Upon leaving said nightmare trick's apartment, have you ever jumped on the first form of public transportation you see, in hopes it will get you marginally closer to civilization?

Question 10: Have you ever said the lyrics to a house, dance, or techno song are "really deep?"

Question 11: Have you ever gotten a bad one-night stand out of your apartment by claiming that your boyfriend is coming back into town that morning?

Question 12: Has your boyfriend ever gotten back into town before you were able to get your bad one-night stand out of the apartment?

Question 13: Have you ever claimed that your trip to the bathhouse was because you really wanted to go, not because you couldn't pick up someone before last call?

Scoring: If you answered "Yes" to one question, you probably answered "Yes" to the majority of them. I don't think you need my help to figure that one out.

Scrumpdiddlyicious!

A *transcript from the April 1 meeting of the local "We Love Leo!" junior high fan club, Buffy Bugg, president*:

Thanks for being here everybody, and thanks to Mr. Baker for letting us meet in the theater between shows. Tonight's going to be my twentieth time seeing *Titanic!* Oh, and I want to thank my uncle Sean and his friend for driving us all here in Mom's minivan.

To handle our old business first: our membership subcommittee decided not to offer fan club membership to Betty. It seems that Betty was overheard by Mary in the bathroom between fourth and fifth period last Thursday saying that Leonardo was, and I quote, "Sort of girly, isn't he?" I'm sorry Suze, I know she's your best friend and all, but if she wants big, sweaty guys, there's a new Bruce Willis movie or something playing next door.

I know everyone really wants to know the results of my research on the Academy Awards. Oh, Heather, this is your first meeting, so I'll tell you. Basically, we just wanted to know why the Academy Awards would nominate a bunch of ugly old guys and *completely* dis Leo. I mean, really. And then give the Oscar to that Jack Nicholson guy. What's up with that? Not only is he really old and ugly, he's kinda creepy. Mom said I'm just too young to understand, like I would ever be old enough to understand that. And Helen Hunt's so cute on *Mad About You*, what was she thinking doing a movie with *him* as her boyfriend?

Anyway, I went down to the library to see if I could find out something about these old guys, and you will not believe what I found. The library didn't have one single Leonardo biography! You'll be happy to know that the librarian told me they would get on the problem immediately. I just can't stand the thought of those poor girls out there who can't afford copies of their own.

Excuse me. *Excuse me!* Yes, these seats are taken. No, you can't sit here, it's reserved for the Leo fan club. Well, you can just go ask Mr. Baker, he'll tell you.

Where was I? Oh, right. Our Leo fund is up to ten dollars and, let's see … thirty-eight cents. We've just about got enough to buy the new Leo biography for Heather. Remember? Heather's mother won't let her spend any more of her money on Leonardo stuff, so we have to pitch in and help out. Oh, Heather, don't cry. We know you would do the same for us.

For tomorrow's meeting, we're all going to my uncle Sean's house. He has a copy of a Leonardo movie we haven't seen, and it's supposed to be a lot better than that *Gilbert Grape* movie, you know, the one where his teeth looked all funny and he acted retarded? This one's called ... what was it? Oh, right, *Total Eclipse*. Leo plays a poet who's also a ... what was it, Sean? Right, a "top."

Whatever it is, Brenda, I'm sure we'll find out tomorrow.

And remember, be ready to vote for your favorite part of Leo. I think I'm going to vote for his hands. What was that, Sean? Oh, wait! The movie's about to start again. Everybody together now:

We love you, Leo!

THE WORLD TURNS
(1999–2008)

Hateful Things

As someone whose religious convictions can most charitably be described as "agnostic," I feel I should point out that when I say Judy Shepard's pivotal role in saving Aaron McKinney from a lethal injection was the most Christian act I've seen in some time, I mean it as a compliment. I'm fully aware that her act could similarly be described as embodying the best teachings of many other religious faiths, but I was raised a Christian, for better or worse, and that remains my primary frame of reference.

Besides, religion in America—at least political America—is a primarily Christian thing. Other religions are generally invoked when Pat Robertson and William Bennett want to make Protestantism appear older than it really is by attaching the prefix "Judeo" to "Christian."

But more interesting than which religious template one might wish to apply to the situation is the fact that, based on what little we can actually know about the full motivations of all those involved in the sentencing of McKinney, in this case vengeance appears to have taken a backseat to the less visceral justice. Contrary to the beliefs of many, the two are not equivalent.

I raise this because now that Matthew Shepard's killers have been sentenced to life in prison, I believe it's a good time to ask how the trial and punishment of the confessed murderers might have ended differently if Wyoming state—or federal—law codified "hate crimes" as an additional category of offense. Perhaps McKinney—and possibly Russell Henderson—would have received additional sentencing to be served consecutively with his life sentence?

Frankly, what's the point?

In the end, McKinney and Henderson committed a particularly heinous crime and have had their freedom taken away by a court of law, the way the justice system is supposed to work in the first place.

One may argue that hate crimes laws are necessary because the Shepard case is an anomaly—a crime brutal enough to capture the nation's attention and with enough resulting media coverage to make finding a jury that would refuse to convict almost an impossibility. Without those aspects, in the context of the average, everyday gay-bashing, a conviction even in the face of a confession would not be so secure.

And that's one of the central reasons I can't support hate crimes legislation.

In rural America—and even in the more "liberal" urban areas—some gay men and lesbians still decline to report physical attacks and assaults, some for fear of being exposed as homosexual, others in the belief that a fair trial would be unattainable. Regardless of right-wing ranting about judicial activism, the courts are not the havens of justice for gays and lesbians that we might—*should*— hope for them to be.

"Gay panic" defenses often work. If Judy Shepard had not exhibited the benevolence to spare McKinney's life, many believe that the gay panic aspect of his defense would have at least spared him the death penalty.

If juries outside the Wyoming media circus are willing to convict a man of far lesser charges, such as manslaughter or simple assault, because the victim "made a pass" at him, why should we believe they would be willing to convict someone on a concomitant hate crime? Or that judges would apply increased penalties based on a perpetrator's homophobia?

The idea that hate crimes legislation will "send a message" is easily dismissed: politicians routinely cite the "deterrent effect" of the death penalty for its use in brutal murders, the drug war, or whatever criminal activity has right-wing Republicans up in arms at the time. And we all know where that's gotten us (to the point of wanting to execute children, in case you missed it). It's vengeance dressed up as policy because vengeance is easy, justice is hard.

Whether you call it "sending a message" or the more clinical "deterrence," the idea that hate crimes legislation will in some way prevent the bashing and killing of gays and lesbians depends on the fallacy that the law in and of itself is a protector. Laws are worthless if the society they govern refuses to enforce them or only does so sporadically, as shown by antiquated and unenforced laws from decades ago that seem odd to today's sensibilities, yet remain on the books.

Is hate immoral? Certainly. I'd even go so far as to call it evil. Hate underlies most of the atrocities of history, whether global, national, or personal. But hate alone is hard to punish because we're all human. We all hate sometimes, maybe just a little bit, maybe a whole lot.

But criminal actions—the infliction of suffering and pain and death—are punishable if and when a society agrees that "equal protection under the law" does indeed apply to everyone, gays and lesbians and bisexuals and transgenders included. And getting there won't be easy, no matter how much legislation is passed by politicians who wish to appear sympathetic by casting a symbolic vote.

Symbolism, like hate, is easy. Justice is hard.

Out With It

I was thinking the other night, as I'm wont to do, that if I ever opened a bar, sex club, or other such gay establishment, a really good name for it would be "The Buckets." Sure, on the face of it, it sounds like a supremely stupid name for a business that caters to the social needs of gay men. But I would be able to promote it with the slogan, "Come by The Buckets!"

I would get a big kick out of that.

This is one of the many reasons I can safely say that I will never be nominated to serve in a president's cabinet or the Supreme Court. Well, that along with the fact that I have no practical experience as a judge, or an administrator of intrastate transportation systems, or managing national currencies in a volatile world market, or other such things.

Then again, lack of practical experience has never really been a barrier to long political careers, as almost-President Bush is proving with his nostalgia tour of the Reagan and Poppy administrations. Hell, he's even reaching back to the Ford administration.

Our entire nation is about to be handed over to the cast of *Grumpy Old Men*.

Anyway, the quadrennial bloodletting of presidential nominees is well underway. This confirmation process is one of those political procedures that makes me queasy as yet another person is put through the combination microscope-and-meat-grinder, yet leaves me breathing a sigh of relief when particularly egregious fools are denied powerful positions.

If you don't pay very much attention, it may even be tempting to feel pity for the favorite Republican martyr, Robert Bork. Even I had a little bit of sympathy for the man who lost his bid for the Supreme Court until I read his screed *Slouching Towards Gomorrah*, which revealed him to be a screaming maniac.

I certainly sleep more soundly now that he's living in obscurity. Bork makes Clarence Thomas look like a reasonable choice for the Supreme Court.

Some candidates manage to self-immolate before the Democrats can pour the gas and light a match. The rigidly moralistic Linda Chavez seems to have violated two rules of the cabinet selection process that would appear self-evident even to someone with the brainpower of a small pile of rocks.

First, don't lie about your relationships with errand-running illegal immigrants who lived in your home.

Second, don't ask your neighbors to lie about it to the FBI. It's too easy a target for any of them who may have a beef with your ongoing lackluster lawn care.

See, you have to be up-front about your past. If you're honest, even if you don't get the job you won't have to call one of those embarrassing press conferences where you whine about how mean the media are for the reporting the fact that you're a big fat liar.

It's not that hard to do. Here, I'll give you an example:

I, Sean Bugg, have engaged in sexual activities with another man and/or men that were illegal even after the repeal of the sodomy law, said sexual activity involving one or more of the following: a stick of butter; public and/or semi-public commercial establishments, including those most definitely not catering to sexual desires of customers; what are euphemistically referred to as "room deodorizers"; and a bottle of Log Cabin maple syrup. No, the Log Cabin syrup was not a political statement either for or against the gay Republican movement.

I just happened to be out of Mrs. Butterworth's at the time.

Free to Be

Perhaps I don't understand the "professional sports player as role model" thing because I never got into football, basketball, or baseball as a youngster, beyond the expected Little League participation. My athletic role models, such as they were, happened to be individual tennis players, both male and female. My goal in following the careers of these tennis titans, such as McEnroe, Navratilova, Evert, and Wilander, was to make my game more like theirs, to be a better tennis player. Although I did have a crush on Wilander that induced dizziness whenever I saw his picture.

The point is: I wanted to play like them, not be like them.

These days, I don't even follow tennis all that often, and the main reason I have knowledge of professional sports at all is because I have to sit through the sports news before I can hear the weather in the morning. But I've learned enough from that to not be surprised to hear that a professional baseball player has shown himself to be a complete jerk by the mere opening of his mouth.

Most everyone has probably heard by now about John Rocker of the Atlanta Braves and the interview in *Sports Illustrated* in which he made disparaging remarks about foreigners, gays with AIDS, and other such things. There was some uproar, some clucking of tongues, and the forces of social opprobrium moved to declare Rocker a bigot—and rightly so.

But then the commissioner of baseball stepped in and ordered that Rocker undergo a psychiatric evaluation, setting off a nice little wave of apoplexy among "anti-P.C." commentators. And, as much as I hate to admit it, they have a point. A small point that only applies in this particular instance, but a point nonetheless.

Should major league baseball be able to punish an individual player for voicing outrageous and bigoted comments in a widely respected (outside of the swimsuit issue) publication? Sure. He was, in effect, speaking as an employee (or perhaps representative) of the organization, and his actions reflect on the organization. All in all, it's a positive step forward that they consider such a transgression worthy of punishment.

But should Rocker be sent to the shrink to be diagnosed? No. Designating stupidity, ignorance, and generalized bigotry as a mental illness doesn't strike me as a particularly good recipe for a happy society.

It helps to remember that one person's ignorance is another person's bliss.

Essentially, everyone has the right to be an asshole. Which is a good thing, because if being an asshole were illegal and, for example, I were in charge of determining the definition of "asshole," the problem of overcrowded prisons would be even worse than it is now. And, as I've interacted with thousands of people over the course of my life, I'd probably end up arrested myself.

So, my feelings on this are pretty much the same as my feelings on hate crimes legislation (which I oppose): you're free to be as hateful of a bigot as you want, but be prepared to pay the price if you commit a crime against anyone you hate (or don't hate, as the case may be).

Thoughts and emotions are just too difficult to regulate by law, as we should know since, "Love isn't a crime."

What's more interesting to me, however, are the cries of "therapy nation" arising from some of the right-wing commentators. They've seized upon the Rocker case to make their point that America is sinking into a morass (as always) in which therapy replaces the legal system.

The *Weekly Standard* recently ran a piece about drug courts, bemoaning the use of drug treatment therapy in place of criminal sanctions. And hey, how can we ever make use of all these new prisons being built if we don't throw every penny-ante offender and addict in the slammer? Also, given the magazine's track record, we can safely assume that the article's opening picture of a transgender prostitute was as hatefully homophobic as it appeared to be.

Anyway, using therapy to help people overcome their addiction problems and reenter society is a threat to American life as we know it. To provide therapy is to coddle the criminal, and we can't win the war on drugs if we help people stop taking drugs.

Funny how therapy seems like such a good idea for many of these people when it happens to be preceded by the word "reparative." But those homosexuals are a different story. They need to be helped so that they can be brought back into society as decent citizens, and everyone should support those fine organizations that offer the helping hand of heterosexuality.

Consistency? What's that?

It's the problem with trying to have it both ways.

Big Bangs

I 'm not a big fan of July, a month both hot and loud. Sure, August is probably a bit hotter than July, but enough people get the hell out of town that things run a little quieter. Thanks to the annual patriotic celebrations, the July heat is punctuated by the continuous bangs and pops of firecrackers, which sound like gunfire and makes me look like an idiot as I walk my dogs and dodge imaginary crossfire.

Isn't one night a year enough for all the little monsters to blow their fingers off with illegal gunpowder products? Use 'em or lose 'em is what I say.

When I was a kid (he said wistfully), I had a healthy fear of fireworks. A lot of that fear came from a book I read about a young boy who goes blind when a firecracker accidentally blows up in his face. The book taught me about the dangers of fireworks in much the same way as my fifth grade bus safety film gave me nightmares for two weeks (not to mention making me afraid to be within fifty yards of one of those big yellow monsters).

When it came to the idea of things blowing up in my face, I was a pretty suggestible kid. The only fireworks I remember being allowed to set off without direct parental supervision were "snakes"—those little black pellets that, when lit, produce a curling ash. Looking back, I see that it was only a bit more exciting than watching a cigarette smolder in an ashtray, but it was pretty cool at the time.

The other thing I worried about blowing up in my face was a car battery. One of the gas companies at the time was running car safety spots on TV, such as "don't tailgate," "don't speed" and all those other bad habits that people seem to think are new just because we call them "road rage" now.

Anyway, one of the spots showed how you could accidentally cover yourself with battery acid if you hooked up jumper cables the wrong way.

I interpreted this to mean that every time you jump-started a car, you had a fifty-fifty chance of searing your face off. This may not have been the most productive belief for me, given that I spent so much time in my father's auto body repair shop, where jump starts were a fairly common occurrence. Every time the cables came out, I took off like a little bat out of hell.

I suppose it's the nature of kids to misinterpret or overestimate the importance of information received. I also believed that if I looked at the arc from an electric welder for more than a half a second or so, I'd go blind. Not that everything I misunderstood dealt with my imminent blinding. For example, I misread the instructions for some feminine hygiene product (don't ask) and spent a confusing period of time convinced that babies were delivered through a woman's armpit.

A much more interesting method than the cabbage patch, you have to admit.

You're probably wondering by now, "What does this have to do with the Fourth of July?" Don't worry, I'm wondering the same thing.

I suppose it's this: grilling and barbecuing, those staples of the Fourth of July cookout, can be frightening if you think about it too much. I've seen big piles of charcoal started off with gasoline. And I've seen what happens when someone gets the grilling order reversed and throws the gasoline on the charcoal after it's been lit.

It ain't pretty.

So, my barbecuing fears center on the possibility that the fire will flow up the stream of lighter fluid and back to the bottle, thereby blowing my hand off, or that a giant glob of grease will explode out of a burger or hot dog and—you guessed it—blind me.

In all, it's probably for the best that I prefer baking. It's easier than becoming a vegetarian.

So, if there's a lesson to be learned, it's that whether you're barbecuing or setting off fireworks, try to make sure that your guests leave the celebration with the same number of digits and limbs they came in with.

Scout It Out

Not being the most outgoing or athletic kid when I was growing up, I occasionally found myself shut out from what the other kids were playing, whether a game of kickball or some other shenanigans on the playground. On a few of these occasions, a well-meaning teacher, parent, or other authority figure stepped in and told the other kids to let me join in.

This was not something I considered to be a fortunate development. The only thing worse than being an ignored sissy was being an ignored sissy who needed a grown-up to make the other kids play with him. It didn't matter that I hadn't sought out adult intervention and would, in fact, have rather done without it. Instead, I would feel self-conscious, which would inevitably lead me to make some mistake like completely missing a kick, and the other kids would feel resentful, inevitably leading them to some retributive action like tagging me out with a ball to the head.

These are some of the memories I've been flashing back to since the Supreme Court decision last week that found in favor of the Boy Scouts of America and its policy of banning gay scouts and scoutmasters from its ranks. It's as if the grown-ups have decided, perhaps even reluctantly, not to intervene on this particular schoolyard.

Although I'm probably stretching a bit too far when I include Justice Scalia, a perpetual bully on the subject of homosexuality, in the set of "grown-ups."

The appeal for government intervention in ending the Boy Scouts' discriminatory practices has been one of those "gay issues" that drives me up the wall, mainly because gay and lesbian political organizations always frame the issue in such a way that it becomes a de facto test for homophobia: if you don't agree with it, you're a hateful homophobe.

I'm certainly no homophobe, self-hating or otherwise, so I naturally take some exception to that framing. I just happen to be one of those people who believe, for better or for worse, that the government shouldn't be telling the Boy Scouts who it can and can't take as members or leaders of the organization.

That's not to say that I have any particular fondness for the Boy Scouts. The organization's policy of excluding gays from its ranks is discriminatory, unethical, and distasteful. And its treatment of James Dale—by all appearances a model of what a Boy Scout should be—was reprehensible. But just because the Boy Scouts can't see the irony in the fact that Dale and others who were kicked out are more exemplary in their Scout-like behavior than anyone working for the Scouts doesn't mean the government should come in and order them to play nice with people they don't like.

Add to this the fact that there are times when some selective discrimination is, dare I say it, a good thing. For example, if I were in charge of the annual gay and lesbian pride parade and representatives from Transformation Ministries stopped by to secure their place in the parade, I wouldn't want the government coming down on me for laughing while I tossed their sorry asses out onto the street.

While I don't think the government should be in the business of setting membership rules for the Boy Scouts, I wholeheartedly support the efforts of those who convince businesses to withdraw their financial support of the Scouts and groups, such as Scouting for All, that work to change the Scouts' policy (even if most of these groups support the lawsuit approach as well).

Those efforts are social pressures, changing the environment in which the Boy Scouts operates. It's one thing to have the government play authority figure to right a wrong and at the same time foment resentment and anger. It's quite another for the Boy Scouts to slowly find itself becoming disdained and ignored by a society no longer tolerant of idiotic behavior on the part of organizations that want to shape their children.

And that day will come, sooner or later. For all the bluster about the well-being of children, this whole fight has been about the grown-ups squabbling on the playground about who gets to say what's moral and normal.

Fortunately, grown-ups don't last forever. And every year, perhaps every day, fewer kids grow up with the same preconceived hatreds that so tie up their "elders." I don't think it's too Pollyanna-ish to expect them to do a better job.

It may take longer, but my guess is it'll be worth the wait.

Stuck in the Middle

I plan on living to be at least ninety years old.

This may seem an ambitious plan—Jack Lemmon just dropped out before hitting eighty, as did Carroll O'Connor and Chet Atkins.[1] The average lifespan of the American male continues to inch upward, but we have to face the fact that after seventy or so, anything short of a meteor or lightning strike pretty much falls under the heading "natural causes."

Why, then, am I so optimistic about my chances?

At the age of thirty-three, I have three living grandparents. My paternal grandfather passed away in 1999 at the age of ninety-six. I have full memories of three of my great-grandparents, the last of whom died in 1998 at the age of ninety-five. I still have three great aunts on

---

1 A friend of mine insists that celebrity deaths come in threes. It's a difficult theory to prove, given the prodigious output of the U.S. celebrity-production industry. When everyone is famous, someone famous dies every day.

my father's side, and a couple of great aunts and uncles on my mother's.

I come from fairly long-lived stock.[2]

That's no guarantee that I'll be popping corks on New Year's 2057. It's hard to even conceive of the year 2057, without the mind wandering off to futuristic fancies like flying cars and orgasmatrons. And just making it to ninety isn't a guaranteed good thing—not much use being ninety if I can't even remember my own name.[3] But I don't think it's too far-fetched to expect medical science to toss me a few extra years, as long as my HMO doesn't order my death as a cost-saving measure.

Plus, I dodged all the bullets of my youth and came through fairly unscathed.[4] Yes, there could be a bus with bad brakes waiting in my future, but I can't control for acts of man or nature. If I spent my time worrying about which incompetent fool—in a world teeming with incompetent fools—is going to run over me with a steamroller, I would never leave my apartment.

---

2   It could be argued that I have and have known so many of my older relatives because I come from an area of the country where people didn't wait for biological clocks to start tolling madly before making some kids. True, but it doesn't change the fact that if you make past ninety, you're pretty damn old. And proud of it.

3   I speak only for myself here—no need to think I'm hinting at some support for Kevorkian-style euthanasia for Alzheimer's patients or anything. So don't worry, your parents, grandparents and former presidents are safe.

4   I dodged the Really Big Bullet during my far more hedonistic twenties, and I've stopped obsessing about it in many of the ways I used to. Still, sometimes I can't shake the feeling that there's a piece of self-replicating ribonucleic acid out there with my name on it.

So, barring natural disasters, man-made accidents, and the long-term effects of various activities that I've given up (or plan to soon), I think I've got a pretty good shot.

The thing is this: divide ninety by three, and you get thirty. Three segments of life, each thirty years long. In the early segment, you spend a lot of time growing and learning and, if you're lucky, surviving the first few years of having a driver's license. In the late segment, you get to retire and, if you're lucky, survive the last few years of driving.

And then there's the middle. The part I've just started. The segment where I take stock of my life, look around at what I've accomplished, and think, *Holy fuck, I wasted a whole goddamn decade of my life and what the hell do I have to show for it, and how the hell am I ever going to be able to afford to retire anywhere but some shithole substandard nursing home in backwoods Kentucky, and oh my god, I am so fucked!*

I consider this to be my first real mid-life crisis, which is distinctly different in tone and content from all my early-life crises.[5,6] My life has become a weird conglomeration of trying to accomplish all those great things that were expected of me as a kid while, at the same time, fighting

---

5   Essentially, during my twenties: Where's the next party? Are we being seen at the right party? What are we wearing to the party? Is our dealer going to be at the party? Replace "dealer" with "bootlegger," and you pretty much have my teenage years as well.

6   I realize there are forty-year-olds and older who still suffer from these early-life crises. It's them I think of when I ask myself, *Could I be any more pathetic?*

off any indication that I might actually be getting older. These are not compatible impulses for me.

You may be thinking that thirty-three is too early for a mid-life crisis. But if I start now I may be able to get over it by thirty-six or so, obviating the need to buy an impractical metaphorical penis like a Corvette.[7] Instead, I bought a Jeep, which is far more practical as metaphorical penises go. I assured myself I was buying it for the practicality: it's short[8] and easy to park, it's a versatile compromise between a car and a truck, and the four-wheel drive will make it easier to get around the city in the winter.

But if I wanted practicality, I would've bought a Subaru.[9] What I wanted was to look young and masculine and virile and all those other self-images that men idiotically mix up with car ownership.[10]

When I'm not tooling around town with the top down looking cool, reminding friends that I can take them places they need to go *in my Jeep*, and generally being an

---

7   I'm not sure if you can actually "avoid" buying something you can't afford in the first place, but you know what I mean, right?

8   A Jeep Wrangler is short in overall length, but about half of that length is made up by the hood, which easily qualifies it as a metaphorical penis.

9   I briefly toyed with the idea of by a VW Bug, just for the fun factor of driving a car that goes by the same name I do. But that's a lot of money to spend for something that would be amusing for, say, ten minutes.

10 I have been to Capitol Hill, and I'm aware of the masses of Jeep-driving lesbians, so I know that not all Jeeps are metaphorical penises. I think Jeep-driving lesbians are the ones who have secretly admitted that a Subaru is actually a pretty stupid-looking car.

automotive annoyance, I spend my time worrying that I haven't published a novel yet. At twenty-five, this wasn't a big deal. I still had plenty of time to get around to it, and everyone knows that writers don't really hit their full creative stride until after thirty.

While I was dicking around with everything and everyone during my twenties, gathering *valuable life experience*, Dave Eggers was putting together *A Heartbreaking Work of Staggering Genius* and David Foster Wallace was becoming the deserved darling of literary circles.

Fuck, even Michelangelo Signorile has published three books over the past few years—someone who could barely write his way out of a book of Mad Libs has left me in the dust.[11] That's reason enough for a mid-life crisis.

So what do I do about this, other than seething with envy and making snide comments about my contemporaries? I feel guilty. I'm writing more every day than I ever did in the past, but I still think I'm lollygagging, not getting around to writing the stuff that really matters.[12] There's a story to be told about my generation, about the lives of gay men in the new millennium, about the social realities of an increasingly fractured America.

---

11   All this is made worse by the fact that Signorile manages to pass himself off as a "journalist." Just a helpful hint for everyone: a journalist's favorite pronoun should not be "I." And there's no irony in me pointing that out in the middle of a gut-purging, first-person essay. I use the first person to write about myself; Signorile uses the first person to write about others. Quite telling, no?

12   You know, like navel-gazing personal essays.

Barring that, I hope to at least finish my horror novel.[13] And if that doesn't work out, I'll just slap together a few half-assed theories of gay male culture, do some minimal Internet research, and draw some wildly provocative yet totally unsupported conclusions.

Such is the urge to get something done.

And speaking of urges, there's the little matter of my biological clock.

My clock, of course, is completely imaginary—we all know that any old coot can knock someone up.[14] It's simply a practical, self-imposed time limit for when I believe I should accomplish my goal of having a kid.

Yes, you heard me right, I want to have a kid.[15] I mean, if Dan Savage can have one, why can't I?

Actually, I have many better reasons to want a child other than the fact that a gay sex advice columnist has one. But all of those reasons hinge on the simple fact that's

---

13 Okay, that's a pretty cheap and self-deprecating joke, given that the horror genre has produced fine works of both literature and pop culture, as well as absolute dreck. But every genre produces dreck, hence the popularity of the *Chicken Soup* series. And I'll take bad horror over that any day, thank you.

14 Assuming he can find a willing recipient of his sperm, in which case it helps to be rich and/or famous, or in a pinch, Tony Randall.

15 As with everything in life, this desire is subject to change without prior notice. That's why I'm trying to work out this whole mid-life crisis thing now, so I'll be sure about it before actually adopting a child. I can take the Jeep back, but this requires a bit more thought. Oh, and I need to find a husband, too. I'll remember to make a note of that on my list.

illustrated by Savage and all the other gays and lesbians participating in the gaybee boom.[16]

I can have a baby.

When I was growing up as a closeted little homo in the countryside of Kentucky, I early on realized that when I came out[17] it would mean no marriage, no kids, none of the things I associated with the families I saw around me. Those things were like going to Mars—interesting to think about, but something that would never involve me.

These days, with churches that will marry me and states that will let me adopt, I've had to reconsider a lot of the choices I made and goals I set when I was younger. And so I surprised myself[18] by discovering that I actually wanted a family of my own.

But that clock is ticking—I don't want to become a father when I'm fifty or more. When I hit ninety, I don't

---

16 Let's all agree that this is the last time we'll ever use the term "gaybee boom," which is the most idiotic and irritating demographic moniker since DINKs.

17 I knew early on that I would come out—the question was only when would I get the hell out of Kentucky so I could come out. Not exactly an inspiring and uplifting story for today's gay youth, but that's just the way it happened.

18 It sounds trite and clichéd to say "I surprised myself," but the first time I thought *I want to have a kid*, I immediately thought *Where the fuck did that come from?* That's probably not a story I'll share with the rugrats, though.

want to be paying college tuition.[19] To my mind, forty years old seems to be the latest I should bring a child into my life. Which means I have six and a half years to 1) find a husband, 2) talk him into having a kid, and 3) actually obtain said kid.[20]

That's actually about fifteen years of work, but what the hell, it's worth a shot. And for the most part, just being willing to try, being open to the possibility, is enough. And if I accomplish half of what I hope to, I have to believe that will be enough.[21]

After all, there's a Corvette to look forward to when I turn forty.

---

19 And just imagine what that'll be in 2057. Unless we live in a flowery utopia where all knowledge is beamed directly into our heads via cerebral interfaces. Well, except for the knowledge the overlords don't want us to have. I'm just keeping my fingers crossed for the flying cars and orgasmatrons.

20 It's easy to make a derogatory joke—and many have—about heterosexuals and the abandon with which they pop out babies for which they haven't planned or prepared. But adopted babies have to come from somewhere, so the rampant breeding habits of heterosexuals have my full support.

21 This is a lie. I will not be satisfied if I don't accomplish the major goals I've set for my life. It's not going to make me suicidal or anything, but it won't make me happy, and it will all be fodder for my second mid-life crisis, which I plan to launch sometime in early 2011.

Got Love? Tips on Finding (and Keeping) a Boyfriend

Y ou can't escape Valentine's Day.

Everywhere you turn in the first weeks of February, red hearts and teddy bears reproachfully remind you that you should be in love. Of course, in the mainstream media, this is mostly a straight thing, as morning news shows put together their annual stories explaining to straight men how to buy flowers, chocolates, and other such mundane items.

How do these guys get by in the world?

Anyway, after suffering through romantic reminiscing by every heterosexual on television and in print, I've come to see that an important voice is missing from the Valentine's barrage: that of the self-involved, whining, romantically challenged gay man. Sure, *The Advocate* has Dan Pallotta on the cover this week, but I don't know if he's romantically challenged.

So I've decided to step up and fill the gap. Don't say I never did anything for you.

About one year into my last major relationship, my boyfriend and I were drowsily lounging on the living room couch, my head resting comfortably against his chest, and I felt gloriously happy as we basked in the late-afternoon sunlight. Wanting to stretch the moment, I suggested that whatever problems should arise in the future, we should always remember this moment, because relationship problems would be trivial in the face of such happiness.

One year later, I'm alone on the couch and shopping for TV dinners.

So you're justified in asking, "Why should I take advice from this guy?"

Well, I've gone through a lot of relationships over the years, and the one thing I can say is this: I rarely make the same mistake twice. I must be learning something along the way. Like, how to make lots of different mistakes. Let's put it this way: I did it wrong so you don't have to.

Getting love generally involves four distinct phases:

1. Find Love
2. Catch Love
3. Prevent Love from moving on to someone better
4. Repeat

Being a rampantly libidinous homosexual of the type that gives Pat Buchanan the vapors can be helpful in finding potential love. But don't worry, being a slut isn't a requirement (although I've always believed the adage "practice makes perfect"). If gay liberation has brought us nothing else, at least it's broadened the dating pool.

The classic method of hanging out in bars and clubs still works, although surprisingly few people enjoy going out to these places alone. You may want to acquire a couple of friends so when in the bars you can project an aura of, well, friendliness. If that's not possible, just do your best not to look scary (suppressing the urge to mutter to yourself while standing in a corner would be a good start).

If bars are too crowded, smoky, and/or reminiscent of high school for your tastes, try hanging out in Starbucks or one of the many non-corporate and lovely coffee and tea houses that dot our small-business-supporting neighborhoods. Remember, though, caffeine is a diuretic, and running to the bathroom every five minutes is not an effective mate-winning strategy (although it is an effective mate-dumping strategy, but that's for another day).

And if none of this works, just start hanging out on Manhunt. You're sure to trick someone into meeting you sooner or later.

Once you've found a romantic target, how do you capture him? The first thing you have to do is embark on an arduous journey of self-improvement. Hey, if you were such a great catch, somebody would already be in love with you, right?

If your self-image has been pulverized by those evil Washington Sports Club ads, you may be ready to hit the gym, although this may be problematic. When I followed this path, I found myself avoiding the gym until I could get into good enough shape to actually show myself in the vicinity of a weight set. I suspect that there's money to be made in the field of pre-gyms, sort of kindergartens for future gym rats.

Once you've got your body together, you need to work on your mind. Run to the local chain bookstore and buy a few random titles from the self-improvement shelf. Specific titles aren't important, since they all basically recommend loving yourself, walking in other people's shoes, and occasionally acting considerate of the needs of others. You know, all that crap. The point is not to read them, but to arrange them around your house so that your potential mate will see them and assume your status as a kind, gentle, loving man. As décor goes, they're probably cheaper than anything you'll find at Pottery Barn.

Now that you've focused on yourself, it's time to focus on the other guy. Namely, making sure he's gonna be the kind of love that's gonna last.

Speaking from experience, I suggest not dating men who have a tendency to go to jail. This can be a tough thing to predict, unless you find most of your boyfriends through prison pen-pal programs. I'm sure there are a lot of Enron-executive significant others out there who didn't anticipate congressional hearings in their romantic futures. But some signs are obvious. Say, a crystal meth factory in the guest bathroom, which implies more than the occasional weekend twirl.

Regardless, you should carefully peruse your potential beloved's past and present to avoid the possibility of conjugal visits, not to mention the risk of getting stuck in the pokey as an unwitting accessory.

(Okay, stop snickering about "stuck in the pokey." We're all grown-ups here, right?)

Next, avoid dating morons. I know, this sounds self-evident, but it can be tricky. You know how in the whole wide world, there must be someone out there who loves you? Well, in the whole wide world, there's also going to be someone who thinks you're a moron. Actually, probably more than one. So don't be too snotty about this one. Count yourself lucky if you find someone who only occasionally acts like a moron.

Unless, of course, he's both a moron and an idiot, in which case you need to just get the hell out.

Finally, don't go barking too far up the pretty tree. It's not that you don't deserve a sex and romance partner with stunning good looks and a titanically hard body. The problem is, for those unbelievably gorgeous among us, they don't really have anywhere to go but down. Twenty years from now, do you want to wake up to a once-stunning face that's seen far better days, or a once-mediocre face that's aged gracefully into dignity and distinction?

The sad thing is, we all know the answer to that question.

Finally, there's the little matter of keeping him once you've snagged him. A doggie cage in the basement is not the answer.

At least not a permanent one.

First, ignore anyone who spouts inanities like "if you love someone, set them free," an adage obviously coined by someone desperate to get out of a relationship.

Next, mark all the Hallmark Holidays in your calendar, so you'll never forget flowers, candy, lube, or whatever presents tickle your lover's fancy. Given current demographic and economic trends, I give Hallmark about five years before it debuts some sort of homosexual holiday, probably featuring those creepy teddy bears. Be ready for it.

Always know what your partner wants in a gift. Forty-eight hours with an escort may be what you want, but it might not be for him. Stick with flowers, and save the escort for when he's out of town on a business trip.

Which leads to this blindingly obvious yet constantly ignored piece of advice: if you're in an open relationship, make sure your partner knows about it. Otherwise, be a man and accept the fact that you're a two-bit, cheating slut. Not that I'm making any value judgments or anything, since another blindingly obvious yet constantly ignored rule is the one about not being a hypocrite.

Anyway, when it comes to playing around on the side, don't forget that jealousy is a matter of perspective. You may feel just dandy when you're sucking some stranger's dick in the bathroom of your favorite bar, but be overcome with jealousy when you find your boyfriend having dinner with a close platonic friend. The solution is obvious—ask your boyfriend to join you in sucking the stranger's dick. No, wait, I mean skip sucking the stranger's dick and go straight home, do not pass go, do not collect two or three phone numbers. Yeah, that's what I meant.

When you've decided not to cheat, don't forget that you have to keep your lover interested so he won't stray either. Remember all that work you did during steps one and two? Well, it ain't over yet. In fact, it's doubled. You always need to be smarter and prettier and in better shape if you have any prayer of keeping your honey. And if you're tired and cranky from all the work, well that's just the price of love.

So, as this Valentine's season winds down and you contemplate your prospects for the coming year, always remember that with some hard work and elbow grease (metaphorical or literal) love will come your way.

Believe me, if you follow my advice you'll get what you deserve.

It's the Heat. And the Stupidity.

I t's hot, and I'm stupid. I wanted to use some big words to tell you this, but they all seem to be lost in the soupy brain sloshing between my ears.

I hate August.

Chances are, you're feeling pretty stupid, too, right about now. If your name is Mayor Anthony Williams, you're definitely feeling stupid, knowing that you stand the chance of losing an election to perennial write-in candidate Mickey Mouse.

One would think that the month during which members of Congress hightail it home for campaigning and fundraising, the president takes off for weeks of vacation, and the people who think circuit party fan dancing is a valid art form disappear *en masse* to Rehoboth would be the most intelligent month of the year.

Alas, it's not the case. August is the grand culmination (whoa, there's a big word!) of summer's brain drain, the time when you can almost hear brain cells popping over the insistent whine of mosquitoes laden with the West Nile virus.

The normally erudite and invigorating (two big words in a row!) Web sites you read each morning have all gone on hiatus. Reading the *Washington Post*, you get the feeling some sweaty editor is half passed out at a desk, moaning, "I don't give a shit what it says, just fill the damn page."

Believe me, I feel that editor's pain.

August is the cruelest, stupidest month because nothing actually happens. We pretend things happen by releasing reports on things that happened last year. We pretend things happen by whipping the nation into a panic over an epidemic of child abductions, followed by a *mea culpa* that child abductions are actually rarer than ever, followed by a report that the abduction epidemic has spread to England. Al Gore pretends to be news by announcing that he absolutely, positively didn't do nothin' stupid during his loser presidential campaign. And then Larry King interviews the long-dead Liberace's male lover, and you know that we're all literally bouncing through hell in an itchy, woolen handbag.

August is so hot and bad and stupid this year that I now enjoy watching Simon and Paula go at each other like aggrieved drag queens on *American Idol*. I've become so idiotic that I considered getting cable again so I could check out *The Anna Nicole Show*. I'm such a moron that I've decided Vin Diesel is an entertaining and engaging screen presence.

In short, I have become so stupid that I'm an actual danger to American society and culture, as are you. For the good of the our nation, let's lock ourselves away in air-conditioned isolation and have Canada wake us come September.

Just make sure our northern neighbors don't let us oversleep. It would suck to miss the new season of *Fear Factor*.

Go Tell It on the Mountain

I've never really been the vacationing type.

I have a number of handy excuses for this personality flaw. My work schedule generally precludes me from making elaborate travel plans. I don't see the need to travel to some distant beach to sit in the sun and read bad books when I can do that on my couch at home, blessedly free of body-image problems. And the hundreds, even thousands, of dollars required for taking any worthwhile trip could always be spent on other things: books, video games, clothes, kitchen gadgets.

You know, the important stuff.

As a result, my vacations have tended toward the practical, generally the result of tacking a couple extra days on a business trip to Miami or some such. More recently, I've found that I can easily justify vacation-like trips in the context of playing tennis tournaments, which just feels healthier and more productive than touring gay bars and larding up at overpriced restaurants. The added

303

advantage is that my partner, Cavin, plays as well, so we've mixed in trips to New York City, Rehoboth Beach, and Louisville in the spirit of competition.

That was our original plan for the 2004 Fourth of July holiday: a cross-country trip to play the Seattle Evergreen tournament. A late-occurring back injury I sustained put the kibosh on those plans, but with airline tickets and discounted hotel bookings already in hand, Cavin and I decided to make it our first shared, non-tennis-oriented vacation.

And I lived every moment leading up to it in mortal terror that the trip would be the end of our still-young relationship. I'd heard the stories: vacations are the beginning of the end for even the happiest of couples, as the stressors of air travel, sight-seeing itineraries, and petty argumentation conspire to crush true love under the millstone of relaxation.

It should come as no surprise that things started off badly and went downhill. We forgot our pricey digital camera, so were forced to buy a couple of crap-ass Kodak disposables to document our joy. Transcontinental coach flights are guaranteed to exacerbate tennis injuries, and my resulting back pain led me to new heights of self-medication with powerful painkillers and muscle relaxants. Cavin picked up a cold on the way out that stayed for the whole week.

I'm a longtime Seattle lover and had hoped to share my pleasant memories of the city with Cavin. He, naturally, was pretty much an instant Seattle detractor, bemoaning the weather, the sights, and the food in equal measure.

A day trip to Vancouver sounded like an opportunity for vacation salvage. Instead, we couldn't find the sights we planned to see, my back left me spasming and angry in the passenger seat of the rental car, and a large chunk of the trip was spent dealing with U.S. Customs.

Just you try re-entering the United States these days with a naturalized-citizen, non-Caucasian, homosexual boyfriend who left his passport at home.

Then, over dinner at a French restaurant on Seattle's Capitol Hill, Cavin shook his head in frustration and said, "We're such different people."

My terror was justified. We were obviously just one short step away from, "It's not you, it's me."

Then, near the end of the week-long sadistic sojourn, we decided on one more day trip: Mt. Rainier. Trying like hell to pull together a cheerful mood on my part, I popped all but one of my remaining pain pills. (I had to have something left for the flight back.) We scaled the mountain in our rented Buick sedan, the most nerve-wracking drive I've ever undertaken—it's as if they've completely adopted the *Star Wars* design aesthetic of "the higher you go, the fewer the railings." But it was genuinely one of the most beautiful things I've ever seen.

We stopped to admire crystal lakes nestled in the forests below, stood on the banks of old, flood-ravaged rivers, and packed summer snowballs outside the resort hotel closest to the peak. We played at tossing each other off of the mile-high lookout points, and we were actually joking, which was an improvement given that Cavin would likely have tossed my ass off the Space Needle the day before if he had been able to snatch-and-lift me. But when we were up there in the mountain's thin air, things started to feel right again—we could be different people but still be in love. That was when I knew the vacation had been survived.

So, Mt. Rainier is the mountain that saved my marriage. Or, more precisely, the mountain that saved my mutually-exclusive, significant relationship with a person of the same sex, at least until I get around to registering at Williams-Sonoma, court rulings be damned. The grainy Kodak pictures are my little reminder that even when things feel like they're spinning out of control and will never feel good again, things can happen that open your eyes to what's right in front of you.

Home Is Where the Camp Is

In the summer of 2008, the writers at Metro Weekly *wanted to put together a series of essays on the experience of being young, gay, and closeted at summer camp. Naturally, I didn't let my lack of experience stop me from participating.*

Given the theme of the magazine, I'm somewhat embarrassed to admit that I've actually never been to summer camp. Then again, I grew up in the farmlands of western Kentucky, where the abundance of wooded fields, muddy creeks, and giant lakes made the whole idea of camp rather redundant.

All those iconic camp activities? They were just a part of life. I learned a bit of leatherworking in fourth grade. I did ceramics with my mother in a small shop in a nearby town. I learned to shoot BB rifles in sixth grade.

Yes, we shot guns in school. I already said it was Kentucky.

I've never, to my recollection, made a god's eye, though I made an enormous number of potholders during one of my crafty phases (just after macramé and just before rug hooking). I never used a bow and arrow, mostly because I had no desire to hunt deer. But the options for all that and more were always there.

So the idea of summer camp as a place your parents sent you to get you out of the house for a month and expose you to the wonders of the non-urbanized world seemed rather decadent to me. Summer camp was something for the Richie Riches of the world. Given that I considered Richie Rich one of the worst comic book characters in the history of mankind—who wouldn't want to engage in a little class warfare after reading the parentally-financed adventures of that little twit?—camp was not something that I aspired to.

That's not to say that camp was unheard of. With the advent of junior high school came band camp. Unfortunately, aside from some mercifully abandoned guitar lessons, I had no musical talent or desire. Though the rumors of *American Pie*-style band camp shenanigans did lead to a brief toying with the idea of taking up an instrument. A triangle, perhaps.

The other possibility would have been Bible camp. Every summer, a bunch of kids from my church—"bunch" being a relative term in a town of just a few hundred people—would pile onto a bus headed for Gatlinburg, Tenn., or some other exotic and pious location for a week of wholesome, God-lovin' fun. Ned Flanders didn't exist yet, but it darn-doodly-tootin' would've been right up his alley.

Of course, there were some band-camp-like tales that came back, surely apocryphal but still titillating. But tales were all I got, as my parents never shipped me off and I never begged to go. I had my moments of faith as a pre-teen, but never moments that big. I preferred staying home and working for my dad fixing cars at the body shop, where I could occasionally sneak some peeks at the copies of *Hustler* and *Penthouse* that were not-so-well hidden in the paint room.

This, of course, was back in the day when *Hustler* and *Penthouse* were really dirty and had ads for gay porn in the back. It was way better than the underwear ads in the back of *GQ*.

Where was I? Oh, right, summer camp.

The closest I've come to a summer camp experience would be vacation Bible school—known to the cognoscenti as "VBS," which in retrospect sounds disturbingly like a disease involving unnerving secretions and reproductive organs.

Vacation Bible school was simply a week of going to church all day long, but with Kool-Aid and sugar cookies. Brother Pettit would give the morning sermon. One sermon I remember dealt with Sodom and Gomorrah— not the sin of the cities, but the power of God in his destruction of them. See, scientists had actually found the cities in the desert and they had been pounded down into the very earth by His wrath.

Luckily for my tender behind, I hadn't yet developed the agnosticism and bravery to do the "bullshit" cough.

The rest of my Bible school memories really revolve around crafty, summer-camp type things—macaroni art or making a "television" out of a cardboard box and a scroll of paper that told the story of Noah (I was a bit of an overachiever on that one). There was lots of singing about Jesus loving the little children and the circuit-ridin' preacher who rode across the land "with a Bible in his pocket and a rifle in his hand."

And church people wonder why some people think religion is scary.

Anyway, all those traditional summer-camp moments—boating on a lake, going on hayrides, exploring the woods—were just part and parcel of my everyday life. Any night I wanted, I could step outside my house, lie flat on the grass, and stare up at the thousands upon thousands of stars, all crystal clear in a sky unfettered by city lights.

I never knew how much I loved that until I didn't have it anymore.

Book Keeping

Should a walking, talking tree from *The Wizard of Oz* or, perhaps, *The Lord of the Rings*, enter my house, I expect that within a few moments it would collapse into a pile of hysterical tears.

"Oh, the *arbor-anity*!" it would cry.

My house, you see, is filled with paper—paper that has been milled, pressed, cut, tattooed, glued between slabs of yet more paper, and then aligned in an order incomprehensible to a deciduous creature. But what would seem a massacre to my wooden guest is one of my greatest treasures: my book collection.

Okay, "collection" may be a bit of a high falutin' word to describe my books. "Collection" implies some sort of method to the madness: a single-minded pursuit of an obscure author, an unexplainable passion for first editions, a mania for a particular modern literary movement. That's all very high-brow, very cultivated, very *literary*.

My bookshelves, conversely, are filled with titles I just felt like buying at the time. Also filled are the cedar chest in my bedroom, the boxes in my closets, and the floor of my office. If I didn't have the credit card bills to prove that I bought them, I'd swear they were reproducing on their own.

I've been addicted to books since I was in elementary school, when my parents would leave me to my own devices at the bookstore in Paducah Mall while they went about their own shopping business. Such callous disregard these days would land them on *Dateline* to be castigated for their shameful parenting techniques, but, luckily, back then we didn't have Stone Phillips to monitor parental responsibilities, so I was free to browse for hours at a time.

And that's where the monster began. At the time, my parents limited me to one book purchase per trip—perhaps two if I was lucky. These days, however, I control my own purse strings, which means that any trip to the bookstore quickly becomes an exercise in instant gratification.

A biography of John Adams? Ooh, that sounds interesting.

Everyone's talking about *In Defense of Food*. I like food. I should get that.

Cheap horror novel? You betcha.

New translation of a Russian classic? I am so there.

Really, it's kind of sad. My to-be-read pile is actually a multitude of stacks spread throughout my home. At any moment, should I be struck by an irresistible urge to read words from the printed page, I can blindly stick out a hand and grab something. Even if it turns out I've grabbed some half-finished Dean Koontz novel I bought twelve years ago, well, it's good enough for a trip to the bathroom.

I am a little judgmental when it comes to books. I'm *that* kind of person, the one who enters your home and immediately starts looking for bookshelves. I don't completely judge someone based on the content of their bookshelves—anyone who tried to judge me that way would peg me as a crypto-fascist, a radical vegan revolutionary, or an expert on Russian literature, depending on which shelf they looked at. I don't care *what's* on the bookshelves, as long as *something* is on the bookshelves.

I just lied a little a bit there. If someone has just one shelf stocked only with tomes by Bill O'Reilly, Sean Hannity, and Rush Limbaugh, I'm going to make a judgment. But let's just call that the exception the proves the rule.

The sad thing is that sometime in the near future, I know this will become futile as people continue to digitize all the information in their lives. I'm not raising some Luddistic call to save the literally printed word—I am, after all, writing this on an iMac, where I can listen to my entire music collection while keeping an eye on my RSS feeds and e-mail in the background.

But when everyone else has become slaves to their Kindles, I'll mourn the days when the fastest way to a man's (or woman's) mind was a perusal of his shelves. Of course, I'll be the crazy hold out in a house full of paper, rambling on to any and all who will listen about the joys of taking a nap on the couch with a huge, densely written book splayed open across your chest.

It's just not the same with a PowerBook.

Domestic Bliss

When I was twenty-five and at the height of my twinkie powers, the idea of settling down seemed romantic but unlikely. The idea of getting married seemed preposterous. And the idea of living in the suburbs, well, that was science fiction.

Yet here I sit, a decade and a half later, with a ring on my finger, watching squirrels scamper unhindered through my backyard, intent on destroying every tulip bulb and flower bed we've planted. Damn squirrels. If someone were to hand me a button that would instantaneously explode the heads of all those bushy-tailed rats, I would totally press it.

Do you *see* what suburban life has done to me?

I jest. Not about the squirrels, but about suburban married life. It may be ironic that all the things I disdained during my screechy, activist youth have now become the things I value: a car that runs, a house that lacks signs of dilapidation, utilities not on the verge of being cut off.

It's a nice life.

Of course, since it's a shared life, there are things I've had to learn. That's because, according to my husband, I'm an inherently selfish bastard who wouldn't know how to share if my life depended on it. Though he usually puts it more nicely.

Usually.

So my first lesson in domestic bliss was to learn to share. Or, more accurately, to appear to share. Apparently, when you offer someone the last Diet Coke, it makes him so happy that he insists you keep it for yourself because he doesn't actually like Diet Coke. Happiness is easy *and* I get to drink all the Diet Coke.

Some other things I've learned are:

Learn to love to clean.

As an inveterate pack rat with attention-deficit issues, I will never be a fastidious housekeeper. But even something as simple as picking food up off the floor when you drop it can help reduce the blood pressure of a husband who compulsively vacuums behind you.

Be understanding of differences.

Being in a cross-cultural relationship, I've found that our differing backgrounds can lead to some stressful arguments over, say, hosting family events or saving money or driving. These arguments tend to devolve into:

"We're Asian and we do it this way!"

"Okay, honey, this is how *white* people do it and I need you to respect my cultural heritage!"

I think that particular argument was over whether or not to eat lots of cake. Naturally, he decided to have the cake, I decided to eat it. Problem solved!

Learn the language of love.

I don't mean how to whisper sweet nothings at the appropriate moments; if I didn't know how to do that, it's unlikely that I would have ended up married.

What I mean is the age-old and poorly understood skill of hearing what your partner says and translating that into what he or she means. Example: "Oh, honey, you really don't have to be buy me anything" means "Get thee to Saks."

My particular lesson was that when my husband says, "You really don't have to buy me anything," he means, "If you spend any more money, I'll be pissed." He's frugal (see *Be understanding of differences*, above).

Conversely, I've had to learn that "nothing" actually means "everything":

"What's wrong, honey?"

"Nothing."

Uh-oh.

Too bad I can't buy my way out of the doghouse with a trip to Saks.

Create some separate space.

When we first moved into our house, my husband was excited that he would have space to "get away from me." I did not react well to that. We were moving in because we loved each other and wanted to be together, right? We should be spending every evening romantically cuddling on the couch watching Oscar-worthy movies and critically acclaimed cable television shows.

But now that I've been here for a few years, I realize that, hell, I wouldn't mind having some time away from myself either. I can be awfully cranky sometimes.

But while all these little lessons have certainly helped, the best thing for domestic bliss is to find someone who never stops making you smile.

Even when he's complaining that you hog all the covers.

Living Single

I am, at heart, an introvert.

It's not that I don't have friends (I have a few) or don't like people (some of you are perfectly pleasant). It's just that, on the whole, I prefer the company of myself. Aside from seeing my husband, which I enjoy, I can go for days without any significant human interaction—other than the nice woman at the 7-Eleven who sells me Diet Coke—and be perfectly happy. Sometimes it seems as if I'm going to collapse into an introvert's black hole, where no social gesture can escape once it crosses the Evite horizon.

That's not to say I'm taking advantage of the soft real estate market to see if I can afford a private little shack in rural Montana. I do enjoy the company of others. Just not, you know, all the time.

So it's not a complete surprise that I found myself out on the town for my fortieth birthday. It started reasonably enough at a little sushi place with my better half and three

319

good friends. Then we moved on to drinks at a different restaurant, including a few more people.

And next thing I know I'm on the dance floor at a nightclub, alongside a surprising number of guys who, I believe, haven't climbed down off the disco box since 1993.

Obviously, I was feeling a little heady—perhaps even dotty, considering my age—which would explain why I ended up talking some tennis smack with a friend and fellow player who's beaten me on court the last six (or seven) times we've played. And those would be the *only* times we've played. Yet I publicly declared that, come September, I would beat him in a challenge match.

A few points about tennis and me.

It's not the first sport I ever played—like most rural kids in 1970s America, Little League baseball took that distinction. But tennis was the first sport I played that I was really good at.

Not dreams-of-professional-success good, but definitely drive-around-Kentucky-in-the-family-van-playing-tournaments good. I had a great serve, as long as I remembered to get my ball toss high enough. My forehand was adequate, though it would break down under pressure.

My backhand, though—my backhand was a thing of Borg-inspired beauty, if I may say so myself. That was the shot around which I built my game, the shot that gave me a little glow inside every time I hit it.

Unfortunately, I didn't play much in college, and, by the time I moved to DC, I had stopped playing altogether, instead spending my time around guys who danced on disco boxes.

About fifteen years passed before I seriously picked up a racquet again. Even though the strokes came back with some practice, they didn't come back the same. When my mother met some of my tennis friends a while back and the talk turned to my adolescent sports career, she asked me, "Is your backhand still better than your forehand?"

My tennis friends think my mother is really funny.

While my backhand may be a shadow of its former self, rediscovering tennis has been one of the better parts of my post-thirty existence, and not just because I met my husband on court. Tennis is a sport that fits well with my inner introvert.

Most of the world goes wacky for team sports—football, soccer, basketball, baseball—all of which bore me both as a player and a spectator. (I'm not going to say anything bad about rugby, though, lest I unexpectedly find myself at the bottom of a sweaty and unshaven gay scrum.)

Those sports all center on the idea that there is no "I" in "team."

I prefer the idea that there is no "U" in "solo."

On a tennis court, I'm alone. It's an opportunity to solve a problem—whether it's how to beat the player on the other side of the net or how to not beat myself. When I win, the joy is all mine. When I lose, I have no one else to blame. It's a beautifully self-contained, black-and-white scenario—a nice respite from the murky grays of the outside world.

So, come September when I step on court for the match I set up with my own big mouth, whatever the outcome may be, it's nobody's fault but mine.

The Anti-Socialite

You know that friend you have who you can call up at a moment's notice with an offer to catch a movie and be guaranteed to get a "yes"? That friend who's always up for something? That friend who loves to while away minutes, or even hours, e-mailing and texting and chatting about life's oddities? That friend you can't do without?

I am not that friend.

No, I'm the friend who turns down spontaneous offers of celebration because I'm pretty sure I have something important to do tomorrow and I need my rest. I'm the friend who, while standing with you in the middle of a crowded bar, is thinking about the book I'd rather be reading right now. I'm the friend who is not always guaranteed to be thrilled by a surprise visit at home.

I'm that type of friend not because I'm malicious or misanthropic. I actually like my friends, all three or four of them. I enjoy spending time with them, and I even occasionally enjoy meeting new friends. It's just that I like to do so under fairly controlled circumstances.

I'm that friend because I'm an introvert and a bit of a loner. One of the gifts of growing a bit older has been the realization that it's okay if I don't want to spend my life living in the middle of a social whirlwind, that there's nothing wrong with my desire to stay at home on the couch. Or in front of the computer, where I can play a massively multi-player online game like *World of Warcraft*.

Solo, of course.

I have decided of late to be a bit more proactive in my socializing and less of a loner. There are a couple of reasons for this. First, I don't want to end up living in a cave—unless, of course, it has a good high-speed Internet connection. But allowing my loner tendencies to grow unabated may, I fear, turn me into a cranky old guy who snaps irritably at television news shows and writes angry responses to political opinion columns.

Okay, fine, I've *already* turned into that person. But if I increase my actual human interaction, there could be hope for me to return to normal. Or at least stop watching Keith Olbermann.

Second, and more important, I've realized that I'm a loner with a husband. I assume that all couples, after a few years of living together, find themselves migrating into patterns of time together and time apart. Unfortunately, I've begun to realize that I've migrated into mostly time apart.

When Cavin and I moved into our house, he half-jokingly said he liked it because it had enough room to get away from me. Hey, I've lived with myself for years, I can understand the sentiment. But it turns out I'm the one with the little loner nest in the house, from which I emerge to watch *Battlestar Galactica*, but not much else.

So, my spring resolution—it's as good as New Year's to me—is to get out of the house more often, to engage my fellow man, and to embrace the idea that change begins at home. I will respond to e-mails and voice mails and twitters alike. I will make lunch plans which I will keep. I will gladly join you for a festive happy hour to celebrate my new-found sociability.

Just be sure to give me a few days warning. You know how I am about surprises.

Pansy Division

anging around my father's auto-body shop during my summer vacations wasn't exactly the same as hanging out with longshoremen or sailors, but I still learned my fair share of salty language from the mechanics, tool vendors, farmers, and others who decorated the paint-scented air with their creative uses of profanity.

Not that it was exceptionally strong stuff, particularly by today's looser standards. These were the pre-cable days when the utterance of "bitch" on network television would cause nationwide apoplexy.

But the language I did learn was salty enough. "Bitch" was ubiquitous, though usually in the form of "son of a bitch," which was itself often pronounced in the one-word formation, "summbitch." "Hell" was still a slightly dirty word at the time, at least when used outside of a specific biblical context, and so was used frequently. "Goddamn" and "bastard" were common as well, but the rarity of "fuck" taught me that it was best saved for special cursing situations.

Such were the seeds of my grown-up potty mouth.

I heard a lot of other words as well.

Once, when I was in middle school, my father was talking with one of his visitors about a well-known and well-liked local man who, due to a childhood bout with polio, got around with crutches and a specially-outfitted pickup truck. Dad summed up the hardships he had faced: "He's got a poor family, he's crippled, and his brother's a faggot."

At that point in time, I knew what a faggot was and I was pretty sure I was one, though it was my most desperate and guarded secret. That one summer moment in the shop was the most painful thing my father ever said to me, and he didn't even mean it to be.

In the late 1970s, faggot wasn't a dirty word. It wasn't exactly something you'd toss around in polite society, but the atmosphere was such that it could be used without consequence, especially in places like my rural hometown. It was part of the litany I heard throughout my closeted youth: faggot, queer, pansy, pervert, fruit.

Words, of course, change with time. I came of age as a gay man during the early 1990s, still freshly out of the closet and full of activist fire. At that time "queer" was undergoing its retrofitting from slur to slogan. Now that the word has become simply an adjectival adjunct to GLBT, it's easy to forget exactly how big that linguistic battle was.

Many, many gay men and lesbians from the generations before mine argued with great passion that you can't "reclaim" a hateful word that you never owned in the first place. For them there was no pride in using a word that carried so much hurt.

Armed with the self-assurance of youth and newfound freedom, it was easy to dismiss such arguments. Queer wasn't really about reclamation anyway—it was about provocation, goading and prodding straight society on issues of homosexuality. It was about being strong and defiant.

Now it's just another in a long line of words once shocking, now mundane—words that serve better in headlines and advertising than conversation or political arguments.

All this is to say that language changes, evolves. That's the beauty of it. The word has been somewhat neutered politically; if someone of my generation or younger—straight or gay—refers to me as a queer, I'm unlikely to bat an eye.

But if a sixty-something white guy were to call me a queer, I would have much different—and likely highly profane—reaction.

While language does evolve, some people will always be stuck in the past. That's why when North Carolina Gov. Mike Easley (D) praised Hillary Clinton as a fighter who would make Rocky Balboa look like "a pansy," it highlighted what still remains a generational divide for gay men.

A substantial number of gay bloggers and activists dismissed the remark, declaring that "pansy" isn't actually an anti-gay term. An equally substantial number of gay men—I suspect largely my age or older—were surprised at how vociferously some gay men were dismissing the impact of a word which so many of us had experienced as an epithet.

It was surprising to me because we've listened for years now to complaints from activists about the use by young people of "gay" as an all-purpose synonym for "bad." I'm not convinced that we should be holding America's youth to a higher standard than a white, fifty-something, Democratic governor of a Southern state who, it could be argued, should know better.

As political controversies go, the pansy flap is why we have the word "kerfuffle," a commotion without any substance. Anyone who was deciding their vote between Barack Obama and Hillary Clinton on the basis of this one event probably doesn't deserve to be voting.

But it does show that we have to be cognizant of the power of our words and not be too quick to dismiss the fact the some words retain their power to hurt long after they've morphed into common usage.

That said, I look forward to the day I turn sixty-five and some activist whippersnapper tries to explain to me why "faggot" is a term of endearment.

Making Change

Whenever I'm faced with the task of providing biographical information about my life, I have a bit of a language problem. Namely, while I want to say that I was "born and raised in Kentucky," that isn't exactly true.

Technically, I was born in California—Camp Pendleton Marine Corps Base, to be precise. It being the late 1960s, my father had been drafted into the service as part of the country's ongoing fight in Vietnam. Luckily for him (and me), he was discharged shortly after my birth and the newest nuclear component of the Bugg family returned home to western Kentucky.

So, as you can see, it's actually a lie for me to say that I was "born and raised" in my home state. But to say that I was "born in California" implies some value to that experience that simply doesn't exist. My infant self was in the state for a matter of weeks, barely long enough for me to open my squinty little baby eyes. It's fair to say that, barring some unknown molecular and chemical reactions with the sunny California weather, my "experience" had no effect on me.

To make linguistic matters worse, to say "born in California, raised in Kentucky" lessens the importance of my home state and family history—it sounds as if Kentucky were a place my parents up and moved to one day on a whim. Actually, the Bugg family has lived in that part of the country since at least the late 1800s. My grandfather was born there in 1911, when California was just the home of a gold rush and an earthquake. I may be the big gay sheep of the family who moved away to gayer pastures, but I still take some familial pride in our shared history.

So, to avoid fibbing about my biography I have to spend three hundred words or more qualifying and explaining the story, and likely boring the living hell out of the listener. Yeah, I can see you nodding off right now.

I face a similar problem these days when I talk about being married to my husband, Cavin. The conversations usually goes something like this:

"Cavin and I got married last year."

"That's nice. Where did you get married?"

"We had a simple ceremony at home in Virginia."

"In Virginia? Does that count?"

"Well, it's not a legal marriage with a marriage certificate and everything. But the state didn't send in a SWAT team, so I think it turned out okay."

On a basic, day-to-day level, I consider myself married even though I'm not legally sanctioned by the

Old Dominion. Both of our families and lots of our friends came together to help us celebrate a Buddhist ceremony that joined us as a couple. We lit the incense, we drank the tea, and as far as I'm concerned we're married.

Of course, when I say that Cavin and I are "married," people generally assume that we eloped to Massachusetts or Canada to receive some sort of legal imprimatur. Since I'm not personally inclined to start a constitutional crisis by suing Virginia to recognize a California marriage, we haven't planned an immediate return to the state of my birth to legalize ourselves this summer—although I think it's likely we eventually will.

I'm a big believer that in order to change the culture we live in, we have to take the small daily steps that make change happen. Even if my marriage isn't a fully legally recognized civil marriage, it is a marriage—in large part simply because we say it's so. The more any of us refer to our same-sex husbands or wives, the more we talk about our marriages, then the more experienced and comfortable our straight friends and neighbors will become with the concept.

That's the way change spreads. When Cavin and I had our ceremony and reception, I'm fairly sure we were the first at-home wedding party in our Falls Church neighborhood in years. I'm positive we were the first big gay wedding party ever. Some of our neighbors joined us, and I'm sure most others heard about it through regular neighborhood gossip.

Since then, armed with our wedding bands and joint savings account, we've had many more chances to help normalize the concept. My favorite was when Cavin was trying to use my Barnes & Noble discount card and the clerk balked because his name wasn't on the card. "He's my husband," Cavin told him loudly, in front of the queue of customers waiting for the transaction to finish.

The clerk took the card.

Some change happens in big, spectacular bursts of publicity. But most change happens in the smallest things we do every day of our lives. It's not always easy to be precise and honest in our language about ourselves and our relationships, but the effort will always be worth it.

AFTER: A WORLD APART

Cross Cultural

Cooking my first Thanksgiving dinner for my in-laws last year, things were going perfectly—up until I sliced off the tip of my finger.

I was in the middle of making a Vietnamese salad of shallots, cucumbers, and rice vinegar, a nod to the culture and cuisine of my husband Cavin's family. It required the veggies to be very thinly sliced, so I broke out the mandoline to get perfect, paper-thin slices.

I couldn't get the shallots to fit into the mandoline's safety guard, so I held them in my fingers and ran them over the freshly sharpened blade: *swick, swick, swick, swi-AAAIIIEEE!*

Finger cuts being the heavily bleeding things that they are, it looked much worse than it actually was. A few minutes of cleansing water and a tightly placed Band-Aid later, I was back in the kitchen. And I still had to get the shallots sliced. So...

Swick, swick, swick, swi-AAAIIIEEE!

And there went my chance of learning Braille. One of Cavin's aunts staged an intervention and completed the last Thanksgiving side dish without the loss of any more digits.

In my own defense, I had been cooking for two days with only about five hours of sleep. After falling into bed around 1:00 AM after a full Wednesday of baking pies and cakes, I rolled out of bed around 6:00 AM to brine the eighteen-pound turkey and start the complicated giblet-gravy procedures.

My sister, Heather, does the same thing every Christmas. Talking with her about our hectic holiday schedules, it quickly becomes clear what we're doing with our frenzied pursuit of complex holiday menus that combine our old Kentucky favorites (cornbread-sage dressing in my case) with frou-frou and time-intensive recipes designed to impress (cranberry-orange sauce with fennel, anyone?). We're recreating a childhood experience that's only half real in the first place, attempting a Herculean schedule of cooking and organizing that no one in their right mind in our own family would have attempted. Our childhood memories of tables of food and desserts were the result of everyone pitching in with a haphazard array of salads and casseroles and cakes and pies.

Heather and I, conversely, try to exercise strict control over the whole thing. And I know things may be a little out of hand when I put more organizational planning into a Thanksgiving dinner than into the average week of editing a magazine—I have lists, timelines, a sheaf of recipes at hand, an honest-to-god plan of attack to make sure not one little thing goes wrong. Thanksgiving turns me into a dictator with a martyr complex. I still feel guilty for two dessert cheats I was forced into by time. First was a Pillsbury ready-to-roll pie crust instead of my own old-fashioned, flaky, lard-based crust for the pumpkin pie. Second was the use of Cool Whip instead of freshly whipped cream for the pumpkin-gingerbread trifle. When I told Heather what I had done, she said, with only partially mock horror, "You used *Cool Whip?*"

But I'm comfortable with all that, as long as I get to eat me some cornbread dressing. Because, when it comes down to it, the memories I'm recreating may be hagiographic, but the holidays of my youth were filled with actual people eating and drinking and laughing and playing cards and acting like a family.

And that's the experience I wanted—and still want—in my own house. It will never be exactly the same. For instance, pretty much everyone in my house on Thanksgiving these days is speaking Vietnamese, except when someone speaks English to translate for me what someone else is saying about my cooking in Vietnamese.

It may sound overly earnest and woefully un-ironic, but Thanksgiving has gained a lot of significance for me beyond the opportunity to show off around the kitchen. Perhaps it's a function of getting older, but as a gay man who came of age in the eighties and nineties, I'm thankful in many ways to even still be around. I'm even more thankful to have found someone to be around with me.

I try not to spend too much time drawing life lessons from the fact that I've been accepted as Cavin's partner by a family of immigrants, because it's too easy to reduce their lives into a Discovery Channel show. But when you spend some time with people who left behind everything to start a new life here, it's not a big stretch to understand how much you have to be thankful for, whether you owe that thanks to God, Buddha, Allah, or just the cold, hard luck of the universe.

But while that may be the underlying reason for the holiday, Thanksgiving itself in my house was filled with people laughing and drinking and eating. Last year was a big first step in feeling like Cavin's family was my family as well.

And I'll gladly cook for twenty-four hours straight to have that feeling again.

THE END

Breinigsville, PA USA
20 October 2010
247740BV00003B/1/P